Celebrating
the
Emma C. Berry

Lawrence R. Jacobsen

Celebrating the *Emma C. Berry*

The history and adventures of the last Noank, CT fishing sloop
and the people who helped her reach her 150th birthday

Lawrence R. Jacobsen

"All boats have heroic pasts."   — F. Slade Dale

Edited by Penny Newbury

**Noank Historical Society, Inc.
Noank, Connecticut**

Noank Historical Society, Inc.
P.O. Box 9454, Noank, CT 06340
www.noankhistoricalsociety.org
Orders may be placed at *www.amazon.com*

Book design © Markham Starr

ISBN-13 978-1515300809
ISBN-10 1515300803

Printed in the USA

DEDICATION

I am so grateful that people from all over the world come to Mystic Seaport each year and admire Emma, but I worry that as the years go by people will forget that it was Noank who brought her into this world, and Noank who brought her back to us. From the designers and riggers and shipwrights at Mystic Seaport, to neighborhood sailors and volunteers who retrieved her, to local historians and journalists who traveled hundreds of miles to hear stories about her when she was away, Emma's biggest fan club has always been right here, and I hope people continue to remember that. This book is dedicated to them.

A typical Noank family: Roswell Palmer (L) and his wife Emma Campbell (Berry) Palmer, with their children Earl (L) and Roswell Palmer and a smack model, in their yard

CONTENTS

Miss Emma C. Berry, ca. 1870s

FOREWORD

I'd read and heard about the *Emma C. Berry* long before I became involved in her restoration at Mystic Seaport in the late 1980's. I'm a marine architect by profession and had worked at General Dynamics (Electric Boat) in Groton, Connecticut beginning in 1940. After my Navy service I worked at various shipyards around the country and then returned to EB, retiring in 1982. As anyone in the area who loves and respects historic wooden boats can attest, I'd been fascinated with this intrepid little schooner, whose name remained unchanged in her hundred-year lifespan as a sloop, a schooner, a yacht, a cruise boat, and even as a twin screw auxiliary cargo schooner. She survived hard work, extreme weather conditions, neglect and near-destruction, and finally was returned to the community where she was built.

I had visited Mystic Seaport often and knew most of its staff quite well. In 1986 Bill Ames, one of the early trustees at the Seaport, asked me to volunteer in the Documentation Shop; this was right around the time of *Emma's* second major renovation. Those working on this enormous task spent countless hours researching fishing sloops of the mid-1800s in order to bring the *Berry* as faithfully as possible back to her original configuration when she first slipped down the ways in Noank in 1866. The second renovation came after additional research was conducted and included the corrections to the sloop rig and the replacement of the wheel with the historically correct tiller. There were no extant original drawings or plans of this little fishing smack, which was not uncommon, but it was well documented that she originally had a sloop rig. One of the first tasks I was asked to perform was to create a drawing of the sails for the Museum archives, as well as a sail plan to be included in the model of the *Berry*, which became available to the public in 1996 and has remained extremely popular.

Nancy d'Estang, supervisor of shipyard research and documentation for Mystic Seaport, asked me to re-design and make drawings of the rig, mast and ironwork after the *Berry's* 1992 sea trials. Under sail as a sloop for the first time in 106 years, the *Berry* performed, in Nancy's words, "as sweetly as it look[ed]," but it was discovered that the new mast was bending, and needed to be sized larger. With the help of Kevin Dwyer from the Museum I began my own research to come up with some additional information so that we got the spars and rigging as close as possible to what would have been the original configuration.

What amazed me, as I was doing even this small bit of research, was the discovery of the enormous number of people from the Noank area who had been or were still involved in the *Emma C. Berry's* history, from her construction to her ownership and working life to her rescue and retrieval. I had come to know many of those people very well—Maynard Bray, Paul Bates, Charlie Haines, Vic Burdick, Cornelius Shields, Sr. . . . they were all part of this history. Even Robert Landrum, who was a mate on the *Berry* when Captain Dayton Newton was restoring her for Slade Dale in the 1960's, was a high school buddy of mine. I began to see that this history of the *Berry* was also a history of the Noank "family" who was still fond of her after 150 years.

To quote Paul Stubing in his short memoir *Emma Berry*, "she patently reflects and summarizes the design improvements that fishermen and builders had worked out together ever since the 1820's. Handsome of sheer, tall-rigged with mainsail and jib topsails strung from a lofty topmast. . . she looks as if she could hold her own against any competitor yesterday or today."

For those unfamiliar with this well-smack sloop, the last of her kind in the world, and for those visiting the area and hearing of the *Berry* for the first time, I wanted to create a relatively brief and easy-to-follow synthesis from the several large and comprehensive documents chronicling her construction, licenses, ownership, fishing and freight hauling trajectory, and reconstructions. These books, manuscripts and progress manuals are in themselves worth taking the time to enjoy thoroughly, both for their technical detail and their maritime history scholarship.

To present an adequate chronology of *Emma's* career I believed it appropriate to include photos and drawings depicting her as she was in her earliest years. I was able to access many of these photos, as well as other pertinent documents, thanks again to the diligent and exhausting research efforts of Nancy d'Estang; parts of her excellent overview *Reconsidering the* Emma C. Berry, are quoted in this book.

Different regions use different terms when describing certain nautical terms, and I've tried whenever possible to provide a brief explanation of a term that may have different meanings depending on the region. For example, the term "smack" had a decidedly different connotation in Southeastern Connecticut than it does in other parts of the country and in maritime dictionaries (whose entries are still being genially fought over by amateur and professional maritime historians alike). In that vein, I am aware that there may be small gaps in my research and attributions, and I hope the reader will forgive what are probably a few lapses in the citations.

In addition to relying on Nancy d'Estang's and Kevin Dwyer's manuscripts and collected documents, my research, which for this book tried to concentrate on the people who influenced and were influenced by *Emma's* remarkable history, was supplemented by technical papers, magazine articles, historical chronologies, and personal reminiscences by Willits Ansel, F. Slade Dale, Wally Hance, Sam Merrick, Paul Stubing and Everett Knapp, among others. I am extremely fortunate that this scholarship exists, for it has allowed me to frame a short but comprehensive picture of *Emma's* history from her creation to her final trip home in 1969. In this way I hope to demonstrate that *Emma's* longevity was due in large part to the many individuals who appeared at the right time, saw something special in this little fishing sloop, and helped her through the many incarnations needed for her to survive in a rapidly changing world.

Past owners spoke of her with affection that went beyond mere appreciation of her ability to make them a decent living. "For seaman and landlubber alike," writes Paul Stubing, "the beauty and the character of this sailing vessel are compelling. The *Emma C. Berry* seems to symbolize absolutely the heyday that Noank enjoyed in the mid-1800's: maritime technology at its most luminous."

It's common for a commercial vessel to change names several times in its career. But *Emma* always remained associated, I think, with the captain's young daughter who lived in the small shipbuilding village of Noank. It does seem, if one were not a dyed-in-the-wool pragmatist as I am, that all through her life *Emma* was being rescued by people who might have felt she was part of someone's family, and so welcomed her into theirs.

A boat, after all, is just a collection of wood and iron and cloth. But this one continues to delight and intrigue people 150 years after her construction. And so with this book I wanted to pay a small tribute to her extended family.

Lawrence R. Jacobsen
Noank, Connecticut, 2015

A BRIEF TIMELINE OF *EMMA'S* CAREER[1]

1865: New well-smack ordered by Captain John Henry Berry, a Noank, CT fisherman. She was originally a gaff sloop with two head sails (staysail and jib) and a light-weather gaff topsail.

1866: Vessel launched June 8th

1866, Autumn: Purchased by Ambrose E. Lester and others, Waterford, CT

1866-1894: Fishing in Southern New England waters

1869: Purchased by Henry Chapel, fish buyer of New London, CT

1872: Robert Wescote was master

1886: Henry Chapel became managing owner, with Calvin Rathbun as master. This was the *Berry's* last year as a sloop

1887: Receives a schooner rig to facilitate handling by smaller crews

1894-1918: Fishing on the Maine Coast. Homeports: St. George, Thomaston, Rockland

1916: Gasoline engine ("Knox gas screw") installed by Beal prior to his ownership

1918: Purchased by Willis Beal at auction in Portland, ME

1919-1924: Used as a lobster smack, transporting lobsters in the wet-well

1924: Purchased by Milton L. Beal for $100 and a set of oilskins

1924: Second gasoline engine installed (Peerless); vessel operated with two dissimilar engines

1924: Receives some new frames and planking

1924-1931: Cargo carrier between Jonesport and Gloucester and other North Shore ports. Carried salt fish, coal, salt, tar

1931: Purchased by F. Slade Dale of Bay Head, NJ

1931: New sails fitted at Boothbay Harbor, ME

1932 and after: Engines removed, bulkheads, bottom, ceiling and deck replaced

1931-1940: Cruising and cargo carrying off Eastern seaboard. Transported piles and ties from Virginia to New Jersey

1940-1947: [Primarily] out of service due to World War II

1947-1954: Pleasure cruising on the Jersey Shore, Delaware and Chesapeake

1954-1957: Laid up in a dedicated special boat slip in Bay Head, NJ while Slade Dale attended to other interests

1957-63: Unused except for a very few cruises on the Chesapeake Bay; no repairs made

1963: Discovered by Captain Dayton O. Newton of Admiral Farragut Naval Academy

1963-64: Restored by Captain Newton and the *Emma C. Berry* Preservation Committee (ECBPC), composed of faculty and students of Admiral Farragut Academy and interested parties from the surrounding area

1965: Hudson River Cruise to Albany, NY and return

1965: Receives new sails and rigging

1966: Centennial cruise to Noank, CT

1968: Offered to Mystic Seaport by F. Slade Dale

1969: Voyage to Mystic Seaport

[1] Taken in part from *"Flash Facts: Schooner Emma C. Berry"* by George Thornton, 1965, in honor of the Centennial Cruise.

CREW LIST OF BARQUE ACORN BARNS.—This fine new barque left our harbor Wednesday morning. Her crew list is as follows :

Charles Jefferey, New London, Master ; Jason Miller, New London, 1st mate ; Manue Joseph, New London, 2d mate ; Joseph Sylvia, New London, 3d mate ; William White, Frank Lewis, Albert Hewitt, New London, boatsteerers ; John Loughran, cooper, New York ; Henrick Bride, carpenter, New York; John Kelley, blacksmith, New York; Charles M. Skinner, cook, New London. Seamen—Charles Potter. W. H. Stone, J. A. Monroe, G. Fisher, W. H Burdick, A. Laphan, M. Joseph, T. Dean, J. Thomson, J. H. Hall.

MYSTIC.—The steamer Loyalist has been running to New York semi-weekly for some times She leaves Mystic on Mondays and Thursdays for New York, and New York Wednesdays and Saturdays, stopping at Noank each way for freight and passengers. The line is becoming quite popular.

NOANK.—A concert was given at Latham' Hall on Monday evening, by Miss Norie of New London, assisted by several young ladies and gents of this village.

A fine smack, called the Emma C. Berry, was launched from the yard of Messrs Palmer and Latham Friday. The E. C. B. was built for Capt John Berry of Noank, and is about thirty-five tons burthen, old measurement. Her fastening, and, in fact, all of her iron work, is galvanized. She is built in the most thorough manner, and when ready for sea will be a neat and handsome craft.

New London Weekly Chronicle, New London, CT, Saturday, June 9, 1866

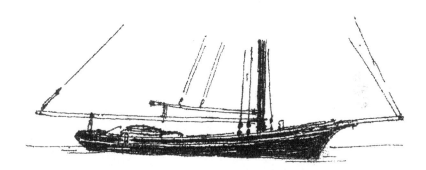

CHAPTER I

Emma and the Noank Fishing Fleet in the 1860s

Since the mid-1700's the village of Noank, Connecticut, at the mouth of the Mystic River, had been an important part of the fishing industry in New England, and was renowned for its construction and repair of many types of fishing vessels. After a relative lull during the Civil War, shipbuilding and boatbuilding activities resumed in Noank and Mystic, and in 1866 the yards upriver in Mystic built a variety of ship types, including the barks *Coldstream*, *Galveston*, *Caleb Haley* and *Mary E. Packard*, and the ship *Twilight II*. The R&J ("Deacon" Robert and John) Palmer yards in Noank, comprising one of the largest shipyards on the Atlantic coast, built the sloop *Almeida*, the half brig *William Mallory Jr.*, and the *Hepsia*.

The Latham Yard, at the end of Latham Lane in Noank, looking out onto Mason's Island. Mystic, Connecticut, date unknown. Note Bailey's Sail Loft, the building closest to the water, where the *Berry's* sails were probably made.

Mystic River showing the Latham Yard, date unknown

The launching ways and remaining elements of the Latham Yard, 2012

One of the most popular fishing boat types of the time, both in New England and as far south as Key West and Galveston, was built in Noank: the smack sloop, a small, single-masted fishing vessel with an internal wet well below decks in which to store the catch. By the time the *Emma C. Berry* was built, the industry was almost a hundred years old, so she had the advantages of some changes in design, with a little more sheer and a narrower bow: "the raking stem flared into the clipper bow; the raked transom and the sheer . . . gave a fine appearance."[1]

John H. Berry

John H. Berry was a Noank fisherman who both owned and captained fishing boats as well as serving as crew on others. In October 1865 he sold his smack *Connecticut* for $2,000 and the following February he commissioned a well smack to be built for $1,275 by John Latham at the Latham Yard located at the "Ledges" (the foot of Latham Lane in Noank).

John Latham built towboats, smacks, and a pilot boat. He and his son James A. Latham had built the smack *Millie,* schooners *Adabelle, Jennie, Manhattan, John Feeney,* and *Phebe*. The Latham Yard was one of the three Palmer yards, which also included the North Yard and the Middle Yard. The North Yard was leased to John Latham from Robert Palmer, with whom Captain Berry contracted to have the new vessel built. The contract was apparently verbal, which was not uncommon in the mid-1800's. Captain Berry named his new smack *Emma C. Berry,* after his daughter, who was then 7 years old.[2]

It was agreed between the parties that the new smack would be two feet longer and a foot wider than Roswell Sawyer's new smack *Almeida,*

Jack Lamb sculling ashore in Noank; the Latham Yard is upriver. Undated.

21

which was being built at the time. This new smack's dimensions were to be 33'2" on the waterline, with a beam of 14'6" and a depth of 5'7".[3] Although other features of *Emma* changed dramatically over the years, her dimensions remained consistent throughout her lifetime.

As already mentioned, *Emma* was originally rigged as a gaff sloop, and her original sails were probably made by the Bailey Loft, which was located right next door to Latham Shipyard.

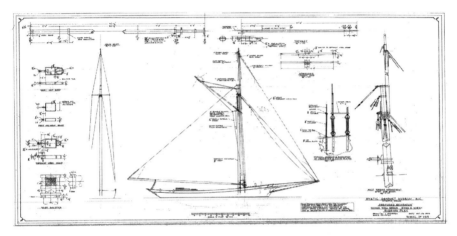

Outboard profile of the *Emma C. Berry*, based on drawings in Willits Ansel's book *The Restoration of the Smack* Emma C. Berry *at Mystic Seaport,* 1969-1971, with corrections made based on additional research by the author. This 1995 plan shows the wheel and wheel box replaced by a tiller, the addition of quarter bits, a stouter topmast and new mast fittings.

It is unfortunate but not uncommon that no original line drawings of the *Berry* exist, and although there was most probably a builders' half model created prior to her construction, that has not been found. As Nancy d'Estang points out in the 1995 Work Progress Handbook that details all of the *Berry's* repairs and changes from the time of her launching, "Although years of research have gone into the quest for details of the *Berry's* original construction . . . it might have to be acknowledged that the type is of medium size, a common work boat—albeit profitable and beautiful—whose construction history chose not to record."[4]

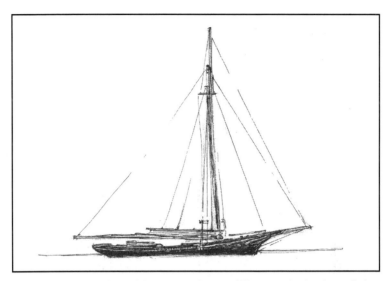

Another line drawing of the *Berry*, from Willits Ansel's book outlining the *Berry* restoration

Combined research by the author and Kevin Dwyer concludes that the Noank smack that most closely resembled the *Berry* was probably the *Manhattan*, built by John Latham in 1855. The design of both the *Berry* and the *Manhattan* were most influenced by the sloops of the Hudson River, some of which were designed and built by William Webb.[5]

The Smithsonian Institute's National Watercraft Collection has in its collection the half-model of the *Manhattan*, donated by L. D. Ashby of

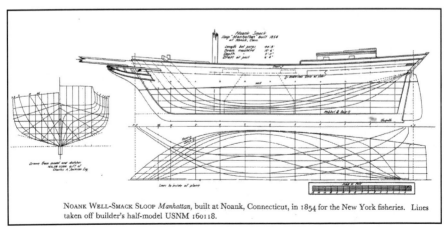

NOANK WELL-SMACK SLOOP *Manhattan*, built at Noank, Connecticut, in 1854 for the New York fisheries. Lines taken off builder's half-model USNM 160118.

Outboard profile of the *Manhattan*, c. 1855

Noank, Connecticut, and from which the lines drawing was made. Their Bulletin says of the *Manhattan* that it was "clipper built and intended as a swift sailer for use in the New York market fishery, [and] similar to sloops such as the *Pronto* and *Viva*, built at New York by William H. Webb in 1842 for the Havana, Cuba, fishery. Noank ship-builders had a great reputation for fine seagoing sloops, having built such craft for the fisheries and for whaling, sealing, and coastal trade since colonial times. The *Manhattan* was built at the time the large sloops were beginning to be replaced with schooners in the New York fisheries, and represents the final development of the Noank seagoing sloop model."

The *Emma C. Berry* was registered in 1866 at Stonington, Connecticut, and was owned and fished out of New London, Connecticut until 1890. However, the registration reveals that John Berry didn't commission her construction for himself alone; she was owned by the following investors: John H. Berry (1/2 owner), Moses Wilbur (1/8), William Latham (1/8), Charles Spencer (1/8), Amos Lamphere (1/8). Ambrose Lester was listed as the licensed Master for the *Berry*—responsible for her operation and her crew. Captain Lester later became captain of Henry Chapel's water boat *Undine* and four months later became 1/8 owner of *Emma*. John Berry sold his interest, along with most of the other investors, and her new owners now included James Fitch, Jr. (1/4), Henry Rogers (1/4), Thomas Rogers (1/4), Amos Lamphere (1/8), with Robert Wescote listed as master. *Emma C. Berry* was owned and fished out of New London until 1890.[6]

History does not reveal or explain Captain Berry's apparent penchant for acquiring new fishing vessels that he himself did not employ in the business of fishing. In 1868, two years after the *Berry's* launch, John Berry ordered a schooner smack to be built by R&J Palmer and named her the *Mary E. Hoxie*. Captain Berry also commissioned James Campbell, the Mystic wood carver, to execute a carving depicting the Masonic Fraternity Square and Compass on the *Mary E. Hoxie's* transom.

With all the obstacles in a fishing boat's path in the mid-to-late 1800's, from weather to collisions to lack of upkeep, *Emma's* survival was a combination of forward-thinking design changes and being in the right place at the right time—or at least staying out of the wrong places. Many of her sister ships were not so fortunate. Scores of fishing smacks succumbed to weather or collision-related events ending in wrecks, sinking, and abandonment. The loss of crewmen to the sea was encountered every day. [7]

Stern view of the *Emma C. Berry* (top) and the *Sylvester*, c. 1889. The *Robbie F. Sylvester* was built in 1887 by Robert Palmer & Sons. The two boats are almost identical, and are of the same tonnage. These photos illustrate the similarity the *Berry* had with many other sloop smacks of her day. Being an effective design, it was naturally a common one. So although the *Berry* was not a unique design, it was the manner in which she was used that helped her to survive where her contemporaries did not.

The loss of the *Manhattan* is one example of the perils of fishing in relatively small boats in the latter part of the 19th century. *Manhattan* was a smack built by John Latham in Noank in the 1850s. She was sailed by Captain Jim Davis and his brother Charles. One year, Captain Charles Davis was "drift fishing" in Vineyard Sound (a dangerous practice) when they were drawn into a rip current and a green sea—a large wave with no foam crest—swept her decks. Three men were washed overboard and never found. Captain

John Berry's schooner *Mary E. Hoxie.*

Davis brought the badly damaged smack back to Noank--alone. She entered the harbor with a flag at half-mast--a sign of death at sea. The accident earned her the nickname "The Old Coffin." [8]

Misfortune seemed to continue to follow the *Manhattan,* for she was abandoned on the mud flats on the Mystic River in Noank where she remained for many years, her timbers plainly exposed at the low water, becoming a threat to navigation and a reminder of her past tragedy.

Other Noank smacks suffered equally ignominious fates much closer to home. An early illustration shows the *Jennie* awash on the Noank waterfront. *Annie* was wrecked on the rocks at Watch Hill.[9]

Not only the Noank smacks but other working vessels as well met their demise during those years. The 246-ton whaling bark *Acors Barnes,* built in

New London for Williams & Barnes in the same year as the *Emma C. Berry*, was destroyed in an Arctic ice pack in 1875, just nine years later.

1866 saw another local ship casualty when the steamer *City of Norwich*, en route in April from Norwich, Connecticut to New York, collided with an unnamed schooner, then burned and sank off Huntington, Long Island. Eleven men were lost, along with a cargo valued at $1 million.

And in a cruel and sad counterpoint to the story of *Emma's* continued survival, her first owner, Captain John Berry, was later lost at sea. Like many fishermen from southeastern Connecticut, he signed on as a crew member to boats that fished in southern waters during the winter months.[10] John Berry was one of ten crew members of the *Feeney*, fishing off Savannah, Georgia, in April

The wreck of the *Jennie* on the left, and the sloop *Annie* aground at Watch Hill on the right. No photos exist of the *Annie* before she was wrecked.

1889. As the *Feeney* began its return trip north, Captain Ebbets reported that "when we left Savannah, we were caught by a storm and blown 500 miles out to sea. Hove to for nearby 20 hours. At one time when the *Feeney* was on a port tack under a small storm trysail she went over on her beam ends and seaman John Berry, who had been at the wheel, was lost overboard . . . ." [11]

Several years before Captain Berry's death, however, *Emma* was making headlines in New London and along the eastern seaboard, thanks to her design and a change made in 1886 by Henry Chapel that would set her apart from other smacks and go a long way towards keeping her alive.

The *Acors Barnes* beset in an Arctic ice pack

Endnotes

1 Willits D. Ansel, *Restoration of the Smack* Emma C. Berry, introduction. For an interesting discussion of the true difference between "smacks," "sloops," "cutters" and their various uses, I recommend the online site *Ships' Nostalgia* (www.shipsnostalgia.com), in which amateur and professional maritime historians pull together vast bodies of research to try and make sense of the different terminology used for different types of ships over time. The discussion regarding smacks is notable for there not seeming to be consensus on whether the term "smack" referred to the size or cargo capacity of the vessel, or if it referred to the wet well and rigging.

2 Further testament to *Emma's* wide-ranging popularity is found in the McHale Family Genealogy, in their entry on Emma Cecilia Berry (no apparent relation): "The [Mystic Seaport] museum maintains that Capt. John Henry Berry, 48, of Groton, Connecticut . . . had it built in 1866 and named for a daughter, (Emma, 10 at 1870 census). Family lore contends it honors our Emma Cecilia Berry, born 1868, or perhaps her mother, Emma Cecilia (Hartman) Berry." *http://www.mchale.com/berry/emmahart.htm.*

3 Deacon Palmer kept extensive journals and lists dates, times, amounts to be paid, and dimensions of smacks and other boats to be built in the Palmer Yards.

4 Nancy d'Estang, *Work Progress Handbook*, 1995.

5 Howard Chapelle, *The National Watercraft Collection*, 1960.

An unidentified fishing smack wrecked at the dock in Noank, c. 1940

6 United States National Museum Bulletin #219, The Smithsonian Institution, Washington, D.C., 1960, p. 267.

7 See E. Everett Knapp's unpublished manuscript, *Smacks of Noank*, for several chapters on storms and tragedies that beset the smacks and schooners of Noank in the 1800's, specifically Ch. 6: "Great Storms," p. 118.

8 The *Mystic Press*, August 29, 1863, Courtesy of Robert S. Palmer; also Ben Rathbun et al, *Noank: Celebrating a Maritime Heritage*, p. 97.

9 Ben Rathbun et al. *Noank: Celebrating a Maritime Heritage*, p. 98.

10 The smack *Annie* is not to be confused with the sandbagger sloop *Annie*, built in 1880 in Mystic by David O. Richmond for Henry H. Tift and used for competitive racing. The sandbagger *Annie* was donated to Mystic Seaport in 1931 and was the first vessel in its collection of watercraft. In 2004 she underwent an extensive restoration, documented in Museum logs, to return her to her original configuration.

11 William Peterson. *Mystic Built*. 1989: Mystic Seaport Museum, Inc.

12 Kevin Dwyer. *Noank Well Smacks and the Fishing Industry.*

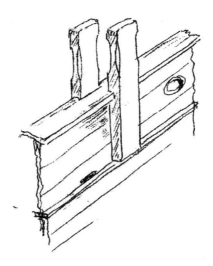

CHAPTER II

The New London Connection and Henry Chapel's Change of *Emma's* Rig

Three miles west of Noank at the mouth of the Thames River, New London was once one of the world's busiest whaling ports. Settled in 1646, it was the region's largest town for over two hundred years. During the mid to late 1800s, there were 100 vessels fishing out of the Groton/Noank area, with 57 of them out of New London.[1]

The waters of Long Island Sound from Fishers Island to Plum Island, however, were full of paradoxes. While the local fishermen, whalers and boat builders toiled in their respective business activities, the privileged classes used the same waters for their summer pleasure. The New York Yacht Club, for example, maintained a clubhouse on Pequot Avenue in New London, and the Sound and Gardiners Bay were the sites of countless sailing regattas. In 1899 the America's Cup defender *Columbia* passed by Plum Island as part of what the *New York Times* called "the greatest fleet of pleasure craft that ever sailed together from New London, and by far the greatest feat of the day was the run of the *Columbia* from Fishers Island to Great Gull Island, in which she averaged almost 13 miles [per hour]."[2]

Fishing Fleet in New London Harbor, 1880's. From 1865-70 about 100 vessels fished out of Groton. (from Charles Stark's Groton, Conn. 1705-1905). In 1860 there were 51 vessels fishing in New London, growing to 75 in 1870.

One of New London's more prominent citizens at the time was Henry Chapel, a Montville, Connecticut native who operated a thriving fish market in New London around 1860, after fishing in smacks at a young age and then going on to became a captain and part owner of several vessels.

Among the many successful fishing vessels owned by Chapel was the *Dexter*, built in Mystic, Connecticut, by Dexter Irons in 1840. Chapel was also half owner of the sloop *John Dexter* in 1867. In 1873, Chapel had a tugboat built for himself and named, appropriately, *Henry Chapel*. And in 1885 he added two water supply boats to his fleet: the *Annie Sherwood*, followed by the *Undine*, mentioned in the previous chapter.

The *Undine*, built by A.D. Story at Essex, Massachusetts, in 1881, had a 5,200-gallon fresh water capacity and was under the command of Ambrose Lester, who had been a one-time 1/8 owner of the *Berry*. Captain Lester and the *Undine* could possibly have supplied fresh water to the US Navy frigates *Galena, Ossippee,* and even the USS *Sabine*, during their Spanish American War period tours at New London and Fishers Island in 1898-99.

The yacht fleet racing at the NY Yacht Club Buoy off of New London, CT

The water boat *Undine,* owned by Henry Chapel

Henry Chapel had been friendly with Robert Palmer, Jr. for years and in 1878 the schooner *Chapel Bros* was built for him by R. Palmer and Sons Company of Noank.

Fish.

HENRY CHAPEL & SON,
Wholesale and retail dealers in all kinds of
Fresh Fish, Lobsters, Clams, Oyster and Scallops.
Fresh water for shipping. First-class pleasure boats for parties. French's Wharf, near Whaling Bank, New London. Orders received by telephone, and delivered with promptness.

Henry Chapel's Fish Market Advertisement, from the New London Day, May 24, 1883

In 1870, Chapel's fish market was located at Frenchman's Wharf in the rear of Whaling Bank on the Thames River. His advertisement stated he was a "Retail and Wholesale Dealer in All Kinds of Fish and Lobsters."

That same year, Chapel purchased the *Emma C. Berry* from joint owners Ambrose Lester (1/8), James Fitch (1/4), Henry Rogers (1/4), Thomas Rogers (1/4), and Amos Lamphere (1/8). Robert Wescote was the Licensed Master/ Captain at the time. After Chapel's purchase, he held a 5/8 interest and Henry Brown held a 3/8 interest in the *Berry*.

The Fulton Fish Market. In this photo, taken around 1875, two Noank boats are seen waiting at the dock: the 49-ton *Maria*, a Noank sloop (5th from the right) and the 33-ton schooner *Isabella* on the far left. Both were built in Noank at the Latham Yard, *Maria* in 1865 by R&J Palmer.

The Noank fishing fleet was heavily dependent on the Fulton Fish Market in New York, and when crews had long periods of good weather and substantial catches, those who owned wet well vessels bypassed Chapel and headed directly to New York where they could get better prices. Henry Chapel also depended on the Fulton Fish Market to purchase what he could not sell locally; he would ship it by rail to New York, no doubt at some expense.

For the next 16 years the *Emma C. Berry* worked as a smack sloop, although during that time fishing sloops began to change to schooner rigs. Many historians agree that one of the main reasons to switch from a sloop to a schooner rig was the ease in handling several smaller sails. Instead of reefing the big mainsail of a sloop, a schooner's sails could selectively be lowered during a gale, thus allowing a smaller crew to handle the vessel.[3]

It is also quite probable that during the *Berry's* time in New London her tiller was replaced by a wheel and a wheelbox. Although the exact date is

The *Emma C. Berry* rigged as a schooner, c. 1934, looking like she did in her early days, on the Chesapeake

unknown, it is certain she arrived in New London with a tiller and when she went to Maine in 1918, she had a wheel and wheelbox.

Always a shrewd businessman, Henry Chapel had *Emma* re-rigged as a schooner in late 1886/1887. It is likely that either the E.P. Beckwith Shipyard, adjacent to Chapel's fish docks, or the nearby Crocker/Davidson yard, was responsible for the construction of her new spars and rigging. [4]

The last registry of the *Berry* as a sloop-rigged smack was in 1886 when she was 20 years old. Henry Chapel sold his fish business to the G.M. Long & Co. in New London that year (it was later located in Groton on Thames Street), but retained ownership of the *Berry*, which received a new license as a schooner in March 1887. [5]

Many accounts of *Emma's* success as a fishing schooner were reported in local newspapers as she fished out of New London and Noank for another twenty years:

"Schooner Emma C. Berry with cod and haddock for G.M. Long & Co. arrived today." (1887)

"Emma C. Berry arrived in Noank with a good fare of cod and haddock." (1888)

"Schooner E.C. BERRY arrived Noank with 27 swordfish - July 9, 1888, and July 18, 1888, with 19 swordfish."

"Schooner Smack E.C. Berry sailed on a cod fishing cruise - November 12, 1889."

"Schooner E.C. BERRY arrived today with 300 codfish to G.M. Long & Co. - March 25." (1889) [6]

The *Berry* was just one of many fast, well-built vessels with an active, productive crew fishing out of Southeastern Connecticut during that time. E. Everett Knapp's unpublished 1931 manuscript offers a detailed testimonial to Noank-built smacks and their crews.

The Noank built smack MANHATTAN made one great record never equaled in the history of smacks. Captain Jim Davis left for Nantucket Shoals, got a full fare of cod, sailed to New York, sold his fish, and back to Noank all in 3 days. He had fair wind to the fishing ground – fair to New York and then fair wind back home to Noank. A steamboat could have done no better.

The Noank built smack FULTON, [with] Captain Elisha Fish, was fishing on Cox's Ledges east of Block Island. She was caught in a hurricane when a square rigger was lost in sight of them. They took the big anchor and stowed it down in the cabin to make her ride easier, and she came thru all right. If there is any ship built better in a sea way and gale than our fishing smacks, she hasn't been seen in these waters.[7]

The *Berry's* success as a fishing, lobstering and swordfishing vessel was also due to the many local captains and licensed masters who chartered her while she was owned by Henry Chapel. Those frequently mentioned in registers or local newspapers, and referred to in Appendix I, include Walton Potter, who chartered the *Berry* in 1881, Edgar M. Slate, who captained her in 1882, Francis Slate, and Robert Sylvester Watrous, in 1885.

In 1891, the *Berry* was still owned by Chapel although she was homeported in Mt. Desert, Maine, and Charles F. Morton was listed as master. She was back in New London, however, in 1892. But Maine was in her future.

Henry Chapel had listed the *Berry* for sale as early as February 18th, 1887 in the *New London Morning Telegraph*. She was again listed for sale in the February 4, 1892 *Morning Telegraph*. Then in 1894, Charles F. Morton and E.L. Bramhall appear in the records as *Emma's* new owners; she had returned to Belfast, Maine, to continue, briefly, her work as a fishing schooner before her new career began.

Endnotes

1 Charles Stark, *Groton, Conn. 1705-1905.*

2 The *New York Times*, August 9, 1899.

3 Kevin Dwyer, *Noank Well Smacks and the Fishing Industry.*

4 Kevin Dwyer, *Noank Well Smacks and the Fishing Industry.*

5 Nancy d'Estang, *Works Progress Handbook, Section H.*

6 These papers included the *New London Day*, the *Connecticut Gazette*, the *Niantic Herald*, the *New London Chronicle*, the *New London Telegram*, and several small local newspapers.

7 E. Everett Knapp, *The Smacks of Noank*, 1931.

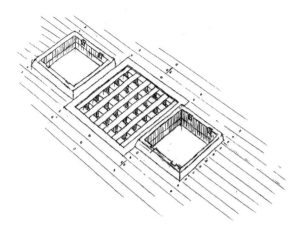

CHAPTER III

Emma Goes to Maine

The *Emma C. Berry* saw many owners and many changes during her 28 years in Maine. A year after her transfer to Morton and Bramhall she was sold again, this time to Carni Connor and six others, and was then operating from Thomaston, Maine, with a fishing license. Except for a return to New London between 1892 and 1893 she remained in Maine until 1931, when a fortunate relocation saved her life.

It's important to keep in mind the changes that were happening in the fishing industry at this time. Advances in electrical and mechanical infrastructure produced a year-round abundance of local ice for safe transport of fresh fish to market, and transport itself was increasingly comprised of both rail service and engine-powered vessels.

The emergence of power brought on the eventual decline of nearly all sail-driven commercial vessels, including Noank fishing smacks.

However, despite these challenges, *Emma* remained productive, being used for a few more years as a fishing vessel, and with her wet well she transported live lobsters and other cargo between ports in Maine. The Merchant Vessels of the United States lists an 8 HP gas engine installed in 1916, this being the first of *Emma's* two engines, and was installed by George Beal, who would later become her owner. [1]

The earliest known photo of the *Emma C. Berry* docked at the C.H. Beals Wharf, Beals, Maine, c. 1920

Former Mystic Seaport Shipyard Supervisor Maynard Bray's 1969 interview with F.W. (Will) Beal of Jonesport, Maine, is one of a series of fascinating and colorful accounts by former owners of the *Berry*. Will Beal was the first person in the Jonesport area to own the *Berry*, buying her at auction in 1918. He took advantage of her wet well and used her as a lobster smack, collecting lobsters at Machiasport, Eastport, Cutler and Lubec. When lobstering was light she was used for handlining or pollack fishing on German Bank and Winter Harbor. George Thornton, who wrote a short history of *Emma* in commemoration of her 100th birthday in 1966, reports that during that time "young Lino Simmons blew out her mainsail in an effort to return to Jonesport in time for a Saturday night dance." [2]

40

The live lobsters in the well took a toll on *Emma's* hull and in 1924 Will Beal abandoned her on the shore of Beals Island. For two years *Emma* lay more or less derelict, "filling and draining with the tide." [3]

In 1926, however, Milton Beal (most likely a cousin) purchased the *Berry* from Will for about $100 and floated her across Moosebec Reach to his home in Jonesport. There she was hauled out and with help, Milton patched her up, removed the wet well and replaced some planking. [4] Still, her hull was far from perfect, her sails were torn, and her rigging damaged.

Emma's fishing days were over, but Milton Beal successfully used her as a coaster during the early days of the Great Depression, transporting coal, salt, dried fish, and a number of other commodities between Rockland, Bangor, and Jonesport. Her topsides were painted green, with the bulwarks, above the deck, painted black. It's interesting that while in Jonesport the *Berry* did not have topmasts or davits. [5] Apparently their first appearance came during a 1934 restoration by F. Slade Dale. By the time *Emma* was donated to Mystic Seaport in 1969, one of the great challenges was determining which amenities were original to the 1866 smack and which were added later.

In 1926 *Emma* was owned by Milton (2/3 share) and his brother George Beal (1/3 share), with George (of Machias, Maine) listed as master. George purchased his brother's shares sometime after 1927, with Milton making quite a profit. A second gasoline engine, this one 12 HP, was installed in 1931. These two engines figure prominently in articles *Emma's* next owner, Slade Dale, would write for magazines such as *Yachting* that describe in entertaining detail his ongoing infatuation with the *Berry*—and his absolute loathing of those engines.

Even with Milton Beal's extensive repairs, *Emma* was considered "used up" and within a couple of years was again left languishing on the mudflats until she was chanced upon in 1931 by F. Slade Dale who was searching for "a picturesque old boat with a keel." He found her not only a picturesque boat but, as he describes in great and entertaining detail, the boat he had been dreaming of since he was a boy.

His written accounts tell of his hearing stories of the *Emma C. Berry* ever since he was a young man in Barnegat Bay. He reports that he'd been told she was "as fine a smack as ever worked the banks, with more than her share of seagoing virtues." [6]

But she was a wonderful vessel of course, for Captain Joe Tilton had been her skipper, and Captain Joe never went to sea in anything but the best vessels afloat; he said so himself.[7]

And though Slade Dale had never seen her, he had always revered her, "though where she hailed from, or what she was, or where she was built, we never knew." But in 1931 he came upon her in the middle of the night and *Emma* was saved once again.

The *Emma C. Berry* in 1931, just after her trip from Maine and arrival in Bay Head, New Jersey

Endnotes

1 Nancy d'Estang, *Work Progress Handbook*, Section E.

2 George Thornton, *"Emma's Epic."*

3 Nancy d'Estang, *Work Progress Handbook*, Section H.

4 Slade Dale 1933 report in Section W of Nancy d'Estang's *Work Progress Handbook*.

5 Milton Beal in section H of *Work Progress Handbook*.

6 F. Slade Dale, *Old Emma Comes to Barnegat, Yachting* Magazine, 1933.

7 F. Slade Dale, *Old Emma Comes to Barnegat, Yachting* Magazine, 1933.

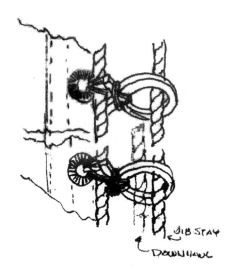

JIB STAY

DOWNHAUL

Chapter IV

Emma Becomes a Lady

"It's not a bad thing to spend your life rebuilding an old boat even if you never finish." — Slade Dale

Slade Dale was neither a fisherman nor in a fish related business. A graduate of the Stevens Institute of Technology, he was a naval architect by training, a member of the privileged class by birth, and a man with unstoppable energy, boundless imagination, and a love for all manner of maritime-related history and activity. He was a yachtsman of renown, a marina owner, adventurer, explorer and prolific writer. Although from the sheltered waters of Bay Head, New Jersey, he was no stranger to deep-water sailing, and even crewed as a second mate on the four-masted schooner *Herbert L. Rawding*.

45

He was experienced in cruising the eastern seaboard from Bay Head to Miami, including daring trips down the Inland Waterway in a twelve-foot Barnegat Bay "sneakbox," and often sailed to Havana, Cuba, in yachts of his own design. In 1929 he was awarded the Cruising Club of America's Blue Water Medal, and in 1934, sailed on the yacht *Edlu* as a member of the winning crew in the Bermuda Race.[1]

After deck of the *Emma C. Berry,* c. 1932. In this photo, *Emma* appears to have just been brought from Maine to New Jersey. Note that the tiller has been replaced with a wheel.

His exploits are recounted in issue after issue of *Yachting* Magazine in the 1930's. He was the quintessential renaissance man of his era, and every exploit recounted in his writing, including the acquisition of the *Berry*, is presented as an historic adventure in which he plays the starring role. It can be argued that in his unfettered enthusiasm for a good story he may have slightly altered the facts about purchasing the *Berry*.

Prior to acquiring the *Berry*, Slade Dale and his close friend Peter Jenness had worked on and sailed many boats, including a yacht called *Postscript,*

Slade Dale enjoyed *Emma* in all seasons.

which occupied the majority of their time until Dale sold her in around 1931 and they "found themselves without a boat." Having proclaimed "a weakness for old hulks" and finding themselves with a bit of cash, Slade took Peter's advice that there was "no use taking a chance on buying stocks and bonds; we might as well blow it on an old boat that we know isn't worth anything."[2] Slade begins this particular story, however, with a memory of listening as a boy to the old captains around the Metedeconk River talk about the old fishing boats, the best of which was a schooner named *Emma C. Berry*. And although Slade never knew where she was or how to find her, she had always, he wrote, lived in the back of his mind as the best, most wonderful of all.

Slade's first acquaintance of the *Berry*, however, probably was not as a boy listening to "Captain Tilton" speak of her, but as a young man serving as second mate on the voyage of the *Herbert L. Rawding*. The trip ended in the port of New Bedford, and Slade's observations and conversations with local captains there framed his vision of his next venture. It was in New Bedford that he saw Captain Zebulon Tilton's schooner *Norris*, and visited with Captain George Tilton (no known relation) and others. He revisited New Bedford with his father to sail sneakboxes back to the Chesapeake Bay, and later met George Tilton again at the New York Boat Show.[3] (George Tilton was caretaker of the whaling vessel *Charles W. Morgan* in the late 1920's.) It was during these visits that the thought of becoming the owner of a schooner captured Slade's imagination; he dreamed of a boat that would "visit many ports and pick up many cargoes" and which "didn't require the upkeep of a yacht."[4]

The schooners in New Bedford were romantic in a hard-working way, carrying pilings and iron and pine tar and heavy construction cargo. Slade Dale was more than a little enamored of this type of rough life—in a theoretical sense.

So in August 1931, after racing first in the Star Boat Internationals at Manhasset Bay, Long Island, and then in the W.C.T. Winlay Trophy Races in Montreal, Slade and Peter set off for the coast of Maine in a rusty Ford, looking for that "picturesque old boat with a keel." A long and discouraging search took them to a nearly endless series of Maine harbor towns: Camden,

The schooner *Lulu W. Eppes*, which carried lumber in the Gulf of Mexico and boxboard in the Chesapeake, was built in 1837 in Kingston, MA as the *Red Rover*, and was rebuilt and renamed by Daniel Eppes of Ellsworth, Maine. She had a hard life, surviving massive leaking and a grounding in Narragansett Bay. It was this type of schooner that captured Slade Dale's imagination, which accounts for his pressing *Emma* briefly--and with near-disastrous results--into this type of service during the later years of his ownership.

Cutler, Machias, Eastport . . . and finally one evening they came upon George Beal's waterfront in Jonesport. They told Beal what they were looking for.

[Beal said] "Let me sell you my boat. . . [she's] in good shape, too . . . I put in some new frames six years ago, a new stern and new planking amidship where she had a fish well . . . ."
"What's her name?" we asked with only casual interest.
"Emma C," replied Beal.
"What!" we roared.
"Emma C," repeated Beal, "Emma C. Berry. Sometimes we call her by her first name, sometimes by her full name, and sometimes just the Berry. And sometimes," he added with more sincerity than salesmanship, "sometimes we call her a damned old sieve." [5]

But as Slade writes, he knew *Emma* was more than that; she was, as he imagined he had heard many times long ago, "the finest little smack off Nantucket."

So after searching amongst dark islands and rock piles in Beal's motorboat, they located *Berry* at midnight, "emerg[ing] from the darkness like an apparition." With a cursory inspection, they bought *Emma* by candlelight. "She was lovely and that was all there was to it; we fell in love with her at sight and have stayed so ever since." They paid Beal what he asked for her and later took possession at the Jonesport Custom House. She continued to be registered as a cargo carrier, and on September 25, 1931, at 65 years of age, the *Emma C. Berry* started her new career.

When Slade Dale purchased *Emma* she was a twin-screw auxiliary cargo schooner, having had two separate gasoline engines installed, in 1916 and 1924. The port engine was a 2 cylinder 4 cycle Peerless, which in Slade's words "meant that chances were two-to-one that it would give trouble," while the starboard one was a single-cylinder 2-cycle Knox, "with only half as many scheduled explosions." [6]

Slade's apparent disdain for these engines is recorded in many of his reminiscences. Discussing the aft cabin, where the Skipper's quarters had been, he describes "two thumping mechanisms of rust and corrosion [that] urged her forward in a din of unmuffled blasts with two jets of flame and smoke coming belching through her cabin portholes." [7]

Slade's sailing and cruising companion, Frank Doyle, joined *Emma's* "crew" in Jonesport for the 3-day trip to Boothbay Harbor to replace shredded sails.

He'd been told to bring a few tools and that he would have to spend a few nights and days below attending to the two engines, since sailing *Emma* at that point was impossible.

Four gallons of gasoline, a quart of oil, a bucket of water (to throw a cupful on the red hot exhaust pipes), and one major breakdown were hourly averages with these engines at their best. And, Slade noted, a hundred and thirty stokes on the bilge pump, to keep afloat.[8]

Emma finally arrived in Boothbay Harbor, and spent a week there awaiting new #8 canvas sails from the loft of John Howell and Sanford Hyler. From Boothbay Harbor the crew sailed the *Berry* to Plymouth, Massachusetts, then began the trip to Bay Head by way of the Cape Cod Canal. The trip through the canal almost led to her demise when failure of her engines caused near collision with bridges and led to her grounding, nearly blocking the channel until she was towed through by canal engineers. Dale's account of the trip is colorful and breezy, but in reality it was probably harrowing and nearly fatal—at least for *Emma*.

After the crew emerged from the canal they sailed to Bridgeport, Connecticut,

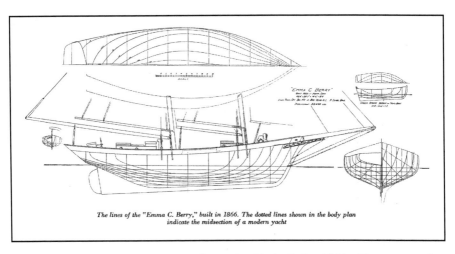

The lines of the "Emma C. Berry," built in 1866. The dotted lines shown in the body plan indicate the midsection of a modern yacht

The lines of the *Emma C. Berry*, drawn by Slade Dale, 1931. His own caption reads *"The dotted lines shown in the body plan indicate the midsection of a modern yacht."* This drawing appears to be the first-ever plans drafted of the *Berry's* hull, which in 1866 was built from offsets taken from her builders' half model, as was the custom. No other line drawing was known to exist. Howard Chapelle's sail plan for her schooner rig, however, has survived; the dimensions of *Emma's* sails never changed during her lifetime as a schooner.

and then on to Bay Head, pumping out water all the way. Still, the journey was leisurely and full of extra sailing time, underscoring Slade's enchantment with *Emma* and his seemingly boundless optimism about her abilities as a sailing vessel (as opposed to a power boat).

Emma C. Berry before her first reconstruction, New Jersey, 1931

Emma docked in Bay Head in October 1931 and was hauled out and stripped clean on the inside. (Her wet well had been removed in 1926.) Her hull was patched and caulked below the waterline, and the hated engines removed. Slade then proceeded to measure her in preparation for creating a lines drawing.

The process of rebuilding *Emma* occurred over the next two years. By 1935, she was completely replanked and redecked. Slade lovingly recounted his discovery and restoration of *Emma* in one of his *Yachting* Magazine articles.

But he also had a vision for her that was quite different from any of his other sleek and splendid acquisitions. Even though he was not a fisherman, Slade always appreciated *Emma* for what she was originally made to do, and noted that while she had many "technical factors in her favor, underneath them all is probably just her seagoing nature which accounts for all her virtues . . ."[9] Slade's idea was for him and his friends to have a wonderful time sailing and cruising aboard her, without too much worry for the near-perfect attention given to other acquaintances' yachts. "Never, I'm afraid, will she reach the pinnacle of rejuvenation which should properly be the climax of romantic history, for we've determined to stop working on her as soon as she's ready to sail again; after that we'll spend most of our time cruising, and we'll fix things only when they give way."[11]

Fortunately, Slade's idea of a carefree attitude towards maintenance, upkeep and daily use equalled far more lavish care than *Emma* had received in all her previous 65 years.

Emma's first reconstruction by Slade Dale, in New Jersey, c. 1932. The *Berry's* decking and framing were completely replaced.

The deck of the *Berry* during her years carrying passengers

Starboard view of *Emma* at her winter berth at Slade Dale's yard in Bay Head, New Jersey, 1944

Endnotes

1 For a more in-depth look at this fascinating man and his many passions and pursuits I highly recommend Sam Merrick's biography, *Slade Dale: the Life of His Choice*, which includes an appendix full of articles he wrote for *Yachting* Magazine recounting his adventures with the *Emma C. Berry* and other yachts he restored.

2 Slade Dale, *Old Emma Comes to Barnegat*, *Yachting* Magazine, reprinted in Merrick, *Slade Dale: the Life of His Choice*.

3 This is verified in his 1928/29 article in *Yachting* Magazine titled *The Log of the Postscript*.

4 Slade Dale, *Old Emma Comes to Barnegat*, p. 120.

5 Slade Dale, *Old Emma Comes to Barnegat*, p. 199.

6 Slade Dale, *Old Emma Comes to Barnegat,* Part II, p. 121.

7 Although this is a wonderful passage in the narrative, Dale is probably engaging in a bit of hyperbole here. The engines certainly could have caused a horrible racket, but since they were fresh water-cooled they would have vented overboard and not into the cabin.

8 The Knox engine was apparently the marine engine of choice in the early 1900s. McLain installed a 2 cylinder 9 HP engine in his new 1904 Friendship Sloop *Estella A*, now a floating exhibit at Mystic Seaport. Also of note: a Knox engine was installed in the new Captain's gig (yawl boat) on the famed 7-masted Schooner *Thomas W. Lawson*. It was reported not to be aboard, however, at the time of the Lawson's disaster. The Peerless engine later became a well-known name in tractors and automobiles.

9 Slade Dale, *Old Emma Comes to Barnegat,* Part II, p. 125.

10 ibid. p.125.

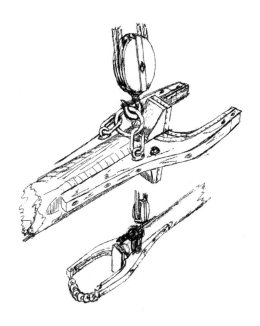

Chapter V

Working for Slade Dale: *Emma* Gets a Tender

The Dale Yacht Basin improved and expanded with the times, allowing Slade to divert funds to continue the long-needed rebuilding of the *Berry*. In his lines drawing, Dale also included proposed stern davits for a dinghy he had purchased prior to beginning his search for *Emma*; he included a drawing of this little boat on the *Emma's* lines drawing as well. This drawing is the first evidence of the *Berry's* having a workboat/dinghy, or a "yawl boat," as they were called during that time. No one writing about the schooner *Emma C. Berry* and the people in her life should overlook the connection of the little workboat to the *Berry*.

Slade had wanted a small sailboat to take to the "frostbite races" at the Larchmont Yacht Club in New York on the west end of Long Island Sound. Frostbiting started in 1932, with Slade Dale, Cornelius Shields, and champion sailor Arthur Knapp among the first participants.[1] In his notes Slade envisioned a "sponge dinghy with red, blue and yellow stripes around it in place of the cotton rope rub rail."[2]

Patience, a Tarpon Springs workboat, length 11' 41" beam 4' 2"

Slade writes that he purchased the little boat in 1932 in Tarpon Springs, Florida from a Greek sponge fisherman. Reportedly she was a workboat on one of the sponge fishermen's schooners. She was heavily built, and fitted with an outboard motor and was often used to tow the *Berry* when cruising, or used by herself as a workboat. She was probably not a sponge boat but a "universal Bahama dinghy: a fine-lined able little boat," as Dale describes her in his 1929 *Yachting* Magazine account of a cruise from Palm Beach to the Bahamas in his previous boat *Postscript*.[3] She was named *Patience* by Cornelius "Corny" Shields, Sr., a racing friend of Slade's, who saw her for the first time at the frostbite races in 1932.

In 1962 *TIME* Magazine editor and avid sailor Maitland Edey called Cornelius Shields "one of the all time greats of American yacht racing, one of the wiliest, most resourceful, and relentless competitors the sport has ever known." [4] This relentless competitor had a very soft spot for the little

Patience stowed in the stern davits of the *Emma C. Berry*, 1941

boat. In his book *Cornelius Shields on Sailing* he wrote, "I was completely taken by *Patience* the first time I laid eyes on her. Every weekend during Frostbite races, I used to admire her while talking to Slade Dale. One day he said to me: 'You know, you love this boat so much, I'd love you to have her.'" Shields said he would welcome a chance to buy the boat but Slade told him "You don't need to buy her--when Frostbiting is over, I will lend her to you, and you could re-rig her and fix her up any way you like and sail her during the summer."[5]

About 1957, at the end of summer, Slade showed his kindness and generosity by selling the dinghy to Shields for just what he paid for her: $85.00. Corny installed a centerboard, and replaced the Gunter rig with a long mast and an Interclub Dinghy sail. He also changed the hull colors: from white with black and yellow trim to a light green hull with yellow and red trim, just as Slade wished, and just as she is now displayed in the Watercraft Collection at Mystic Seaport. *Patience* was donated to the Museum by Shields in 1990.

Cornelius Shields writes of the dinghy:

I love Patience more every year; every year, she gives me more pleasure and satisfaction. To see her jumping at her mooring, exposing that lovely forefoot, is an endless source of delight. [My son] Corny and I do most of the maintenance work on her, with an assist from Toby Brekne, the captain of the Larchmont Yacht Club. She's nailed, which is unfortunate, for the nails have a tendency to rust. Whenever Corny or Toby or I find a nail that has rusted, Toby pulls it out and replaces it with a brass screw. [6]

Sailing Patience is sheer joy. She has the most wonderful motion in a sea you can imagine. She's dry and doesn't throw any water. She has great personality—more than any boat I've ever known—and she's a little tender, so you have to watch her. I take her out on race days, or any other day, and sail around, going out alone on the Sound, sometimes sailing to another harbor to see what's going on there. Patience has countless admirers; wherever I go, people hail me and tell me how pretty she is. [7]

Cornelius "Corny" Shields in *Patience* sailing off Larchmont, New York, 1972

In 1932, after *Emma* was moved to Morton Johnson's Boatyard for a complete rebuilding, she was registered in Philadelphia, Pennsylvania for carrying freight and passengers. Slade used the *Berry* for twenty years just as he had originally intended: for pleasure cruises, some charter cruising, and some freighting. Annual cruises of two to three weeks were made with five or six friends, mostly on Chesapeake Bay.

Emma C. Berry, June 1937 after her complete rebuild, starting a 2-week cruise on the Chesapeake

Slade made at least two separate freighting trips between Norfolk, Virginia, and Bay Head, carrying eight tons of creosoted piling for docks, and railroad ties for his new marina. However, as the *Asbury Park Press* reported on December 29, 1940, "a few ties were lost overboard when hove to in heavy seas breaking over the stern while off the Virginia coast. The opened seams threatened future trips, and *Emma* was deemed too elderly for this form of cargo transport." [8]

Slade Dale's many cruising venues included the canals of the Great Dismal Swamp between Norfolk, Virginia and Elizabeth City, North Carolina.

All accounts indicate that Slade put *Emma* to work hauling freight not because he needed the money but because he was an entrepreneur at heart, and to him, all work was in some measure "fun;" if George Tilton's Cape Cod cargo schooners could do it, then *Emma* could do it, too.[9] It's likely, then, that part of him always thought of her as a workboat despite the inordinate amount of time and money he had invested in her restoration. All his writings indicate a respect for her origins, combined with an almost nostalgic wish to himself be part of a former era.

Here we had an old vessel rich in the sentiment that clings to craft that serve a useful purpose in life, and endowed with physical qualities not possessed by any yacht. Ours was a vessel that wouldn't make us slaves to paint and varnish; we could welcome friends on board with hobnails in their shoes, and we could let the dory bump alongside all night without worrying about the topsides . . . we could chop wood on deck and not worry if smoke from the galley stove smutted up the foresail . . . if we dropped a marlinspike from the masthead we knew it wouldn't go through the deck . . . we'd hang our clothes on boatnails driven into the bulkhead. . . . We'd be one of many struggling little vessels along the seaboard, poorly rigged of necessity and . . . endowed chiefly with a scarcity of cargoes.[10]

Given that Slade Dale was a man of so many talents and interests it is notable that *Emma* held his interest so steadily for so long. Even upon her "retirement" from hauling cargo, it was over twenty years before Slade could bear to part with her.

The *Berry* loading pilings in Norfolk, Virginia for her trip home to Bay Head, New Jersey. She barely survived the voyage.

The *Berry* rests at anchor as the sun begins to set.

Endnotes

1 c.f. Barbara Lloyd's February 23, 1997 article, "Frostbite sailing draws unique breed to icy waters of Long Island Sound," in the *New London Day*.

2 Sam Merrick, *F. Slade Dale, The Life of His Choice*.

3 Slade Dale, *Postscript's Winter Cruise, Yachting* Magazine, 1929, p. 88.

4 Maitland A. Edey, *Sea Dog Eat Sea Dog*, in *TIME* Magazine, July, 1962.

5 Cornelius Shields, *Cornelius Shields on Sailing*, p. 91.

6 ibid. p. 91.

7 ibid. p. 91.

8 The *Asbury Park Press*, December 29, 1940.

9 Sam Merrick, F. *Slade Dale: the Life of His Choice*, p. 22.

10 *Yachting* Magazine, *Old Emma Comes to Barnegat*, Part II, pp. 122-23.

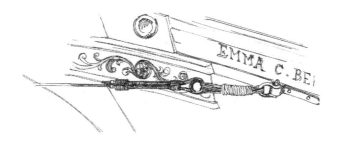

Chapter VI

Another Rescue, and a Birthday Party

During World War II Slade was Captain of a 110-foot subchaser, and later was assigned to the Navy's Bureau of Ships to impart his design expertise to the war effort. So for the majority of the war, from 1942-1947, *Emma* was "laid up--" consigned to her slip at the marina, although immediately after the war and into the early 1950's she resumed cruising up and down the New Jersey coast and in Chesapeake Bay.

Slade Dale stopped sailing the *Berry* in 1956, although sources report that she received a new set of sails that year. But for the most part, from 1957 to 1964, *Emma* remained idle and relatively neglected in a special dock slip at the Dale Yacht Basin, even after he sold the business in 1959.

Talks in 1957 between Dale and Mystic Seaport regarding the acquisition of the *Berry* had been less than fruitful due to the need for an endowment to maintain her afterwards. Still, the Museum remained extremely interested in her recent activities and her condition, since she was built just five miles away in Noank and "probably the only one of her kind in existence."[1]

And by 1957 Dale already was busy with other projects—spending time in the Bahamas, becoming a competitive cyclist, and, on a sailing trip in Maryland, becoming enamored of a 65-foot Chesapeake oyster freighter he just could not live without. He spent upwards of $100,000 converting the "buy boat" *A.G. Price* into a luxury river cruiser that he re-named *Coastal Queen*. This vessel could take up to 6 passengers up the Inland Waterway in grand style.

Just as quickly as she had inspired his passion, *Emma* was cast aside, and in 1963 Dale wrote to Captain Dayton Newton "I now find myself so wrapped up with [the *Coastal Queen*], for a little while at least, that I am not going to make much progress with the *Emma C. Berry*."[2] This was music to Captain Newton's ears, for as a teacher at the Admiral Farragut Academy

The *Coastal Queen* has been impeccably maintained, and many residents of Noank, Mystic and New London had the chance to see her as she participated in the 2012 New York Yacht Club Summer Cruise up the Thames River. While we are slightly defensive that Slade Dale threw *Emma* over for her, she is an amazing vessel and we are delighted she is kept in such wonderful condition.

in Toms River, New Jersey, he had proposed earlier that *Emma* be used as a restoration project for his students.

Once again, 97-year-old *Emma* escaped the fate of languishing on a mud flat. As a licensed sailing master, Captain Newton brought a wealth of seagoing experience to the Academy and its students. A Lieutenant Commander in the Naval Reserve, he had served in the Arctic in World War II. He had also spent 25 years in the Maine coast Windjammer cruise trade with his schooners *Maggie* and *Adventure*.

Captain Dayton O. Newton at the helm of the *Berry*. The yacht-like finishes, complete with bronze wheel and brass binnacle along with fly rail and stern davits, are as she appeared at her 100th birthday celebration in 1966.

Captain Newton's request to adopt the *Berry* for a school project was considered by Slade to be a suitable solution. He agreed that Newton should "take the vessel in hand to do with as you outlined, with entire stewardship for as long as you are actively interested in her personally, though without transfer of ownership."[3]

The *Berry* was then moved to the Academy dock on the south side of Toms River, New Jersey where she underwent an extensive restoration, and in 1965 took a five-week cruise to Troy, New York, and as a "glossy" schooner yacht drew much attention en-route. The trip was reported in the July 5th edition of the *New York Times*.

Meanwhile, back in Noank, all was not complacent; plans were afoot. In an early 1964 meeting of Noank residents considering the formation of an historical society, resident Paul Stubing revealed that he had learned of the existence of the *Emma C. Berry*, owned by New Jersey businessman F. Slade Dale.

Paul Stubing was the first conservator of paintings at Mystic Seaport; his varied career included wooden boat and fine art restorations. He was also a marine watercolor artist, and a lobsterman out of Noank. He agreed to

Two views of the cabin interior of the *Emma C. Berry* as restored by Dayton Newton

investigate the possibility of the *Berry* visiting Noank as the highlight of the opening of the Noank Historical Society. Subsequently, Stubing reported that Slade Dale was even willing to have Captain Newton bring the *Berry* to Noank on July 4, 1966, the 100th anniversary of her launching.

Dayton Newton's 1966 restoration had *Emma* outfitted in "yacht fashion."

For that year, the focus of Captain Newton was to prepare *Emma* for her 100th birthday. When readied, "she appeared in her yacht-like splendor, her topsides freshly painted black and with new gold leaf."[4] The topside color possibly irked Slade Dale a bit, since the black paint was the only part of the restoration he wasn't happy about, *Emma* having always been dark green.[5]

July 3, 1966 marked the *Emma C. Berry's* Centennial Cruise, and she arrived in Noank to help celebrate "an event unique in maritime history. It was reported to be the only time a merchant vessel had returned to the shipyard of her building a century after her launching."[6]

Captain Newton's crew included mate Robert Landrum, able seaman; Arthur Krause, cook; Marcia Krause, seaman; George Thornton, Methodist minister and deckhand; and William Thornton, student. Mr. and Mrs. Krause were high school teachers from Chester, Connecticut. They and Minister George

Left Photo: Donald Singer (R), then owner of the Noank Shipyard, signs the Bill of Lading from Captain Dayton Newton (L) in 1966 for *Emma's* last cargo (a shipment of fiberglass). The *Emma C. Berry* is believed to be the oldest continuously documented vessel licensed to carry cargo.

Right Photo: Robert Landrum (L) presents a commemorative plaque to Donald Singer in 1966 marking the return of the *Berry* to Noank where she was built in 1866.

Thornton had sailed with Captain Newton in Maine aboard his schooner *Adventure*. Robert Landrum, Rev. George Thornton, and William Thornton were with Captain Newton on the 1965 Hudson River Cruise. Robert Landrum was a professor of Mathematics and Philosophy at Rutgers University, a Mystic Academy graduate, and a 1940 Fitch High School (Groton, CT) graduate.

The *New London Day's* Noank reporter, Mrs. Helen Maynard, wrote the following in her column:

Ceremonies on the occasion of the Berry's 100th Anniversary were extensive and will be best described in records and reports by the Noank Historical Society members and Noank community leaders when the Berry's 150th Anniversary of her launch in Noank and the 50th Anniversary of the Noank Historical Society occur on July 4, 2016.[7]

The Rev. Elbert E. Gates was also quoted in the *New London Day*: "The sturdiness of this ship, the fact that she set sails to the seas a century after she first touched the water is a reminder to us of another era who were God-fearing, home-loving, and took great pride in the things they produced."[8]

Emma arrived at the Noank dock in 1966 to her cheering "family."

Endnotes

1 Sam Merrick, *F. Slade Dale: the Life of his Choice*, p. 45.

2 ibid. p. 35.

3 ibid. p. 46.

4 Sam Merrick, *F. Slade Dale: the Life of his Choice*.

5 Everett Knapp's research in *The Smacks of Noank* indicates that all fishing boats prior to a certain date were painted green; after that date they were black. *Emma* fell into the "green" category.

6 Sam Merrick, *F. Slade Dale: the Life of his Choice*.

7 This quote was repeated in several papers including the *New London Day*.

8 Joy Basurto, *Facts from the Past*, the *New London Day*, 2006.

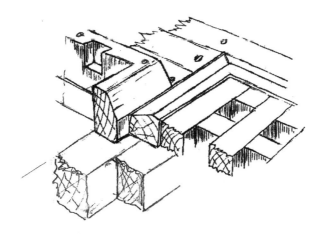

Chapter VII

Emma Comes Home for Good

Following the celebration of the *Berry's* 100th anniversary on July 5, 1966 in Noank, she returned to Toms River, and from there was towed home to Point Pleasant, New Jersey. Then began two years of "discussions and arrangements" between Mystic Seaport and Slade Dale, and in 1968 he formally offered the *Berry* to the Museum. Another year elapsed before the delivery.

Dale paid $743.80 to put her in condition to be taken to Mystic. To assure that she was in fair enough condition to survive the trip, the Museum enlisted Henry Palmer, a marine surveyor from Stonington, Connecticut to travel to the Dale yard in Bay Head and inspect *Emma*.

Mr. Palmer's 1968 survey notes that *Emma* was "in remarkable condition for a 100 year old sloop," displaying "good looks, fair sheer . . . planking surprisingly hard and generally fair." However, his notes also include some disheartening phrases, such as ". . . a few main facts would condemn her as a

The *Emma C. Berry* in 1969, just before Slade Dale gave her to Mystic Seaport

total loss, for any purpose other than what you have in mind." Although her 1935 restoration had included much new planking, she had been repaired in a haphazard fashion for much of her career. Still, Mr. Palmer pronounced her seaworthy enough for the delivery to be undertaken. 1

On June 14, 1969, Maynard Bray, the newly hired shipyard supervisor at Mystic Seaport, along with his wife Anne and daughter Kathy, headed to Bay Head, New Jersey in the Museum's utility boat *Two Brothers*. On June 20, six days after the Bray family arrived and gave the *Berry* a quick paint job, the rest of the delivery crew arrived and got to work rigging the vessel: Paul Bates and Victor Burdick of Noank, Charlie Haines of Mystic, Arthur Krause of Chester, and Michael Sturgis and Frank Young of the Museum's staff. The plan was for Chester Patterson of Stonington and his powerboat *Night Hawk* to tow *Emma* back to Mystic.

The delivery trip was exciting, emotional, and very well documented in third-party articles and first-hand logs and accounts, notably by on-board historian Arthur Krause, with Maynard Bray and Michael Sturgis in an article entitled *The Voyage Home* published in the September 1969 issue of the *Log of Mystic Seaport*.[2]

The ship's logs record in good-natured and wry detail the many adventures *Emma* and her crew survived during the trip. Despite an ancient hull,

This c. 1969 photo shows the *Emma C. Berry* hauled out on the Morton Johnson railway (probably the same railway she was hauled out on in 1931 when she first arrived in Bay Head), prior to making her seaworthy just before her donation to and final trip to Mystic.

overworked bilge pumps and a questionably stable sailing rig, the crew took advantage of every opportunity to sail her, much like Slade Dale had back in 1931, when he first brought *Emma* to New Jersey. And "with *Night Hawk* dodging oil and railroad barges and a strong favoring current, the *Berry* set a sailing record from the Battery to Hell Gate that no New York taxi driver would ever dare to equal."[3]

Because the Mystic Seaport railway could not accommodate the *Berry* until later, she would have to remain afloat throughout the winter, with work scheduled to commence in the spring. She was leaking so badly, however, it was feared she might sink before then. She was therefore hauled out downriver at Mystic Shipyard and under the guidance of its manager, Major Smyth, patched up and recaulked. The first restoration phase began the following spring and is described and illustrated in Willits Ansel's detailed and easily readable account, *Restoration of the* Emma C. Berry.

The launching ceremony of the newly-restored sloop (the work included giving her back her original rig) occurred on May 7, 1971 at Mystic Seaport, where she was re-christened by Mrs. Florence Oliver, the first President of the Noank Historical Society.

The *Emma C. Berry* in Manasquan-Barnegat Bay Canal. Maynard Bray is at the helm; Slade Dale is standing beside him.

The *Emma C. Berry*, free of tow lines off City Island, New York and on her way back to Noank, 1969

Slade Dale wrote, in a letter to Maynard Bray dated June 1971:

It has been especially gratifying that so many people have taken such enthusiastic interest in the vessel's return home. Needless to say, I enjoyed my part in saving the ship through her lean years until rescue came . . .

Sadly, Slade Dale never had the opportunity to return to Mystic to see the

Crew members clockwise: Vic Burdick at the helm, Charlie Haines at work seizing on new ratlines, Paul Bates in the rigging, Maynard Bray at the helm

Berry restored, as he would say, to "perfection in a score of details;" his letter to Mystic Seaport was dated the month he was diagnosed with cancer. He died in October 1972 after a final voyage on the *Coastal Queen*.

The first restoration by Mystic Seaport of the *Berry* (1969-1971) replaced her wet well (which had been removed in 1926) and gave her back her original sloop rig. The second restoration (1995) took care of structural issues and refined the rig so she could be sailed. Although the 1992 sea trials revealed some issues still needing attention, she performed magnificently and certainly looked like she was very glad to be sailing again as a sloop in her home waters.

Endnotes:

1 Nancy d'Estang, *Work Progress Handbook*, section S (surveys).

2 Arthur Krause, Maynard Bray and Michael Sturgis, *The Voyage Home.* Reprinted in *Slade Dale: The Life of His Choice* in Sam Merrick's book and in the fall issue of the *Log of the Mystic Seaport*.

3 All the records and photos from the time that Captain Newton was in charge of the *Berry* were put together by Arthur Krause, who was a crewmember on *Emma* during her voyage to Mystic and also on the Hudson River trip.

AFTERWORD

To see the *Emma C. Berry* impeccably restored to her original configuration and learn more about her history and restorations, a trip to Mystic Seaport in Mystic, Connecticut, is invaluable.

The Museum has lovingly cared for her for over 40 years and offers many special programs that include the history of fishing smacks in the area.

The *Emma C. Berry* is a special part of the Mystic Seaport Watercraft Collection and is a floating exhibit. She appears much as she did when originally built.

Illustrated books, with plans covering her restorations at the Museum's Henry B. duPont Preservation Shipyard are available at the Mystic Seaport Bookstore.

For information, visit:
www.mysticseaport.org

LIST OF ILLUSTRATIONS

JVH: John Van Horn, Jr./F. Slade Dale Collection
MSM: Mystic Seaport Museum, Inc., Mystic, CT
NHS: Noank Historical Society, Inc., Noank, CT

CHAPTER I

Sketch: The *Emma C. Berry* by Lawrence Jacobsen. Author's Collection

Latham Yard. © NHS, #1990.026

Mystic River showing the Latham Yard. © NHS, #1987.005

Latham Yard railway remains, Latham Lane, Noank, CT, 2012. © NHS

John H. Berry. (c) NHS, Palmer Collection

Jack Lamb sculling ashore in Noank. © NHS, #2004.015.010

Outboard profile of the *Emma C. Berry*, by Lawrence Jacobsen, October 26, 1995. © MSM, Daniel S. Gregory Ships Plans Collection, #SP7.6.43

Berry midship, drawing by Willits D. Ansel. Courtesy of Willits D. Ansel

Outboard profile (line drawing) of the *Manhattan*. The National Watercraft Collection, by Howard I. Chapelle, U.S. Government Printing Office, 1960, p. 267

The *Berry* at her winter berth in Mystic, Connecticut. Author's Collection

Stern view of the *Robbie F. Sylvester*. © MSM, #80.41.430

Mary E. Hoxie. © MSM, #1972.882.4

Jennie, Noank, CT, ca. 1872. © NHS, Paul T. Stubing Collection, #2004.015.009

Annie at Watch Hill, RI. Courtesy of the Utter Family

Acors Barnes beset on an ice pack, Robert R. Newell, Whaling Historian

Unidentified fishing smack wrecked at the dock in Noank. Photo by Adrian Lane, 1940. Courtesy of Jonathan Lane

CHAPTER II

Sketch: Quarter Bits by Lawrence Jacobsen. Author's Collection

New London Harbor fleet photo. © MSM, #86-12-29

The yacht fleet racing at the NY Yacht Club Buoy off of New London, CT. © NHS, Paul T. Stubing Collection, #2001.001.020

Undine. © MSM, #80.41.140

Chapel advertisement, The New London Day, May 24, 1883

Fulton Fish Market. © NHS

Emma C. Berry rigged as a schooner. © JVH

CHAPTER III

Sketch: Cargo hatch to the wet well, by Lawrence Jacobsen. Author's Collection

The earliest known photo of *Emma C. Berry*, Beals, ME, c. 1920. Courtesy of Milton Beal

Emma C. Berry upon arrival in Bay Head, New Jersey, 1931. © JVH

CHAPTER IV

Sketch: sail cringle, by Lawrence Jacobsen. Author's Collection

Emma C. Berry after deck, c. 1932. (c) MSM, #1973.496/Ex.coll.: F. Slade Dale Estate

Slade Dale aboard *Emma* in winter. © JVH

Schooner *Lulu W. Eppes,* Ellsworth, ME, watercolor by Victor Mays. Courtesy of Peyton Mays, Sara Mays Hessler, and Jefferson Mays

Lines plan by Slade Dale. *Yachting* Magazine, July 1933, p. 124

Emma C. Berry before her first reconstruction, NJ, 1931. © JVH

First reconstruction, New Jersey, 1931-32. © JVH

The deck of the *Berry* during her years carrying passengers. © JVH

The *Berry* at her winter berth in Bay Head, NJ, 1944. © JVH

CHAPTER V

Sketch—gaff boom and halyard, and reverse view, drawing by Lawrence Jacobsen. Author's Collection

The Tarpon Springs workboat *Patience*, at Mystic Seaport, 2012. Author's Collection

Emma C. Berry with *Patience* in the stern davits, 1941. © MSM, #1973.528/ Ex.coll.: F. Slade Dale Estate

Cornelius Shields sailing *Patience*, 1972 . © James L. Amos/Corbis

Emma C. Berry, June 1937, after her rebuild, Tupper photo, *Yachting* Magazine, p. 48

The *Emma C. Berry* cruising in the Great Dismal Swamp. © JVH

The *Berry* loading pilings in Norfolk, VA. (c) JVH

Emma at anchor in the sunset. © JVH

CHAPTER VI

Sketch –Billet Head, by Willits D.Ansel. Courtesy of Willits D. Ansel

The *Coastal Queen*. © JVH

Captain Newton at the helm of the *Berry*. © NHS, #1998.57.30.6

The *Berry* cabin interior. © NHS, #1988.57.30.21

The *Berry* cabin interior (2nd photo). © MSM, Arthur Krause Scrapbook, #69-5-26-A

Dayton Newton's restoration (stern view), 1966. © MSM, Arthur Krause Scrapbook, #69-5-26-2

Donald Singer signing Bill of Lading, 1966. © NHS, #1988.057.30.18

Donald Singer receiving plaque, 1966. © NHS, #1988.057.30.14

Emma arrival at the Noank dock, 1966. © NHS, #1988.057.30.10

CHAPTER VII
Sketch: Framing at the cargo hatch, by Lawrence Jacobsen. Author's Collection
Emma C. Berry, F. Slade Dale ownership, 1969. © JVH
The *Berry* on the Morton Johnson railway, 1969. © JVH
The *Berry* in Manasquan Canal with Maynard Bray and Slade Dale. Courtesy of Ocean County Historical Society, Toms River, NJ.
The *Emma C. Berry* on her way back to Noank, 1969. © NHS, Victor and Kathleen Burdick Collection, #2008.015
Crew member Vic Burdick at the helm, 1969. Courtesy of Maynard Bray
Crew member Charlie Haines at work seizing on new ratlines, 1969. Courtesy of Maynard Bray
Crew member Paul Bates in the rigging, 1969. Courtesy of Maynard Bray
Maynard Bray at the helm, 1969. Courtesy of Maynard Bray

AFTERWORD
Emma C. Berry as restored, Mystic Seaport, 2010. Author's Collection

APPENDIX I
Emma C. Berry model on display at Noank Historical Society. © NHS

AUTHOR BIOGRAPHY
Lawrence Jacobsen, July, 2015. (c) Markham Starr

BACK COVER
The after deck of the *Emma C. Berry* at her current berth at Mystic Seaport, 2009. Author's Collection

APPENDICES

I. *Emma C. Berry* model by Roger Hambidge, on display at Noank Historical Society

II. 1889 Connecticut Bureau of Labor Statistics report on the value of the catch. Captain R.S. Watrous of Mystic, mentioned on p.163, was Captain of the *Berry*

III. Two views of the 1905 Knox engine

IV. Survey performed on the *Berry* in 1969 prior to her delivery in Mystic

V. 1969 log of the return of the *Berry* to Mystic, by Arthur Krause

VI. List of staff who worked on the 1969-71 and 1987-88 restorations and the Sea Trials in 1992

Appendix I

Emma C. Berry model, constructed for the Noank Historical Society by Roger Hambidge. Roger also assisted with the second reconstruction; he created some of the drawings to ensure that the *Berry* was as close to the original as possible.

Appendix II

1889 *Connecticut Bureau of Labor Statistics* report on the value of the catch.

FIFTH ANNUAL REPORT

OF THE

BUREAU OF LABOR STATISTICS

OF THE

STATE OF CONNECTICUT,

FOR THE

YEAR ENDING NOVEMBER 30, 1889.

———

PRINTED BY ORDER OF THE LEGISLATURE.

———

HARTFORD, CONN.:
PRESS OF THE CASE, LOCKWOOD & BRAINARD COMPANY.
1890.

CAPITAL, VESSELS, CATCH, EMPLOYES, AND WAGES.

Gear and outfit.	Value of catch.	NUMBER OF EMPLOYES.						
		On smacks.	Wages.	On shore.	Wages.	Total number.	Total wages.	
$137,500	*$269,800	577	†$72,125	25	$7,500	602	$79,625	1
70,500	138,800	267	33,375	25	7,500	292	40,875	2
67,000	156,000	310	38,750	....	....	310	38,750	3

THE SWORD-FISH FISHERY.

There are three or four sword-fishing boats that sail from Bridgeport.

Henry Chapel of, New London : Sword-fish average about two hun-dred pounds weight each, and sell at wholesale from two to seven cents a pound.

Captain R. S. Watrous of Mystic: Most of the sword-fishermen run to Block Island breakwater each night. The boats catch one to fifteen fish a day. Good average day's catch is six. There is one sword-fishing boat at Stonington. The season begins June 20th, and ends September 1st.

Edward Clark of the *Mattie and Lena*, Stonington, is a sword-fisher-man.

Samuel B. Pendleton of Stonington: Sword-fish are caught off Block Island from June to September 1st. One smack caught thirty-eight of these fish in one week. These fish weigh from 125 to 450 pounds each, and wholesale at from two to fifteen cents per pound.

The record of one sword-fishing schooner (the *Stephen Woolsey* of New London; net tonnage, 31.10, value $3,200) for the season, June 15, September 7, 1889, is as follows: Made ten trips to fishing grounds between Montauk and South Shoal lightship; caught 19,061 pounds of sword-fish, valued at $940.77; number of persons on vessel, four, including one foreign subject.

---

* A few swordfish included in the catch. † And found. Help all Portuguese, very cheap.

BUREAU OF LABOR STATISTICS.

FISH INDUSTRY — LOBSTER FISHERY — BY TOWNS, CAPITAL, VALUE OF CATCH, AND MEN EMPLOYED.

TOWNS.	Men.	Capital.	Pots.	Value.	Value of catch.
The State, ...	257	$69,462	11,156	$24,825	$95,175
Branford, ...	10	850	300	300	1,100
Guilford, ...	6	600	200	200	790
Madison, ...	20	1,400	700	700	1,645
Clinton, ...	7	1,500	400	500	1,800
Westbrook, ...	15	1,250	450	563	1,540
East Lyme, ...	10	1,762	306	612	2,800
New London, ...	56	14,800	3,000	6,000	15,800
Groton, ...	26	8,675	800	2,200	8,700
Noank, ...	77	35,175	3,700	10,175	54,000
Stonington, ...	26	8,350	1,300	3,575	12,000

THE LOBSTER FISHERY.

Allen B. Ashby of Stonington, sets his lobster pots on trawls, and hauls them in by steam. Lobstering is carried on in Fisher's Island Sound, Block Island Sound, and The Race.

Hamilton, Powers & Co. of New London: The southwest winds which prevailed in July, backed up the great quantities of fresh water that, owing to heavy and continuous rains, was coming down the river. The result was that our fish and lobsters died in the cars at our market.

Samuel B. Pendleton of Stonington: During the heavy storms of September, 1889, the lobstermen lost about all their pots and gear. One man saved five pots out of one hundred and twenty-five. Pots are worth from two to five dollars each. In the summer time the lobstering is done in fifty fathoms, 300 feet, of water.

Edward Waters of Clinton: I set thirty-five to forty lobster pots a day. Caught more lobsters this year than ever before. The average catch each day for five or six weeks was 150 pounds. Have caught 200 pounds a day.

NOTES.—These lobstermen, except as otherwise indicated, employ no help. They use a small boat, 12 to 15 feet long, or skiff, to take up their pots. There are larger and stronger half-deck boats, and therefore more valuable, at the eastern end of the State. The pots are also more valuable from East Lyme to Stonington, as they must be better built and more firmly anchored. Out of Noank go twenty-two small half-deck boats, two steamers, and eight smacks, with a total tonnage of 370, a value of $16,000, and a catch of $94,000. Thirty-three men are employed, with wages of about $150 the season and found, and the number of pots used is 1,200. These totals are included in the Noank showing. The smacks make their catch in "The Race," Long Island and Block Island Sounds. Most of the other lobster fishermen get theirs inshore among the rocks. As lobster pots can be hauled only on slack tide, the boats catch sea bass and bluefish on the quick tide. This catch is inseparable, though not large, and is included in the values in this presentation.

Appendix III

Two views of the 1905 Knox engine.

KNOX C.1905

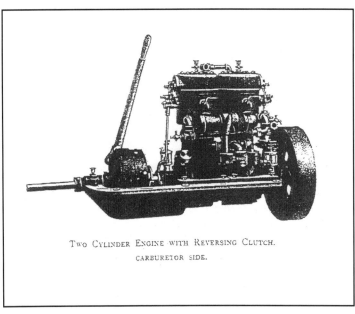

Two Cylinder Engine with Reversing Clutch.

CARBURETOR SIDE.

Appendix IV

Survey performed on the *Berry* in 1969 prior to her delivery in Mystic.

PALMER SERVICE, INC.

Marine Surveying
182 WATER STREET
STONINGTON, CONNECTICUT 06378

HENRY R. PALMER, JR., President
Member Nat. Assoc. Marine Surveyors

March 27, 1969

Phone (203) 535-0147

Mr. Edmund C. Lynch
Marine Historical Association Inc.
Mystic, Connecticut

Dear Mr. Lynch,

       This is a report of survey performed by us March 24th 1969 on the schooner yacht EMMA C. BERRY hauled on a railway at the Morton Johnson yard in Bay Head, N. J.

       As anyone who has seen her out of the water knows, she is a handsome craft, and it was gratifying to note the fine overall condition of her bottom planking. According to owner Slade Dale she was completely replanked in 1935 with 2" juniper specially picked out in North Carolina, and so far as we could determine, it is as sound as the day it was put on.

       Her keel is completely sheathed with copper which extends part way up the deadwood and up to the waterline on the stem and also up and over the graboard rabbet seam which of course prevented any examination of these areas. Apparently the keel, stem and deadwood are original, and according to a caulker who was checking her seams and butts while we were conducting survey the rabbett was a "trifle soft" when he caulked it "about 20 years ago", but he quickly added that the softness penetrated not over three eights of an inch, and that when he attempted to bore some holes in it, he burned out three drills. So it would appear that the backbone is reasonably sound.

       The keel is slightly hogged, however. The yard knew this before she was hauled and so placed her on the cradle so that about ten or twelve feet of her keel stuck out ahead, unsupported. They felt that this was the proper way to haul her and were pleased that they had done it this way, because if she had been supported on her ends, her keel would not have touched the bearers amidship, thereby imparting great strain on her.

       The caulker discovered a few seams that needed recaulking, but otherwise she was as tight as could be. Every butt below the waterline is covered either with sheet lead or wood. We had the caulker remove one of the latter (screwed in place) and the seam beneath it was perfectly sound. These

93

-Mr. Edmund C. Lynch-

"patches" were apparently installed to keep the seam compound
from dropping out. Sometimes the plank ends become chafed, or
the fastenings fail to hold them firmly in place with the result
that they "work" when the boat is underway, allowing compound to
fall out and expose the cotton. This is more often apt to happen
on boats where planking is butted on the frames, as on the
EMMA C. BERRY, than on boats whose butts are securely held together by thru-bolted butt blocks.

When the BERRY was replanked in 1935 she was also re-
framed (according to Slade Dale) although many of her original
timbers were left in. At that time new bilge stringers were
installed along with an entire new deck and deck beams . So in
effect she was new in 1935.

Currently she is suffering from bulwark stanchion and
covering board problems. At least three stanchions to port and
ten to starboard are rotted out, and around most of the rotted
places the covering board is rotting too. This condition has
caused the sheer plank on the starboard side to let go at one
butt(and perhaps in other spots). Both knightheads are rotting.
These are commonplace problems in this type of construction,
and not serious--providing the condition is rectified immediately.

Her topside planking, cap rails, transom planking and
decking appear structurally sound with moderate waste, wear and
tear. Transom frame was new in 1935 and from within looks fine.
Stern post looks to be relatively new and the horn timber feels
perfectly sound. It rained hard during much of the survey, but
decks showed no signs of leaks. She was, however, sweating rather
badly. Deckhouses, sills and tops all appear sound.

She has no true sheer clamp or shelf, but instead is
heavily ceiled. The top ceiling strake on the port side is broken
or rotted at 7 points, and the one to starboard at 2 points. But
so far as we could determine, the ones below it are OK.

Her bilges are wet and muddy, but her floors and frames
seem remarkably sound. They are soft on their exteriors for a
depth of a quarter of an inch or so, but are sound beyond this,
a normal characteristic of old wood in bilges.

Slade Dale came aboard during the survey--the first time
in six years. He explained that he had loaned the BERRY to a Captain
Newton who wanted to fix her up and get her in good condition, and
who was willing to do this completely at his own expense simply
for the pleasure of so-doing. According to Dale, this man turned out
to be enthusiastic but not particularly skilled, and although he
did the boat no harm and actually did it a lot of good, some of his
efforts were misdirected and not always authentic. For one thing, he
installed a mahogany monkey rail aft, a "yachtish" galley below,
and changed the paint job from green hull and white masts to black
hull and oiled masts. But Dale himself in 1935 or so did a not-too-
aunthetic job of joiner work in the cabin, installing a good deal of

-Mr. Edmund C. Lynch-

machine-carved trim work. But authentic or not, the workmanship is excellent, and the main cabin could be extremely handsome if it were cleaned up and repainted.

Her main mast has a rather severe twist in it, but it and the foremast appear sound. Standing rigging is in good shape: wire, deadeyes and lanyards (although the latter might better be replaced if she is to be sailed North). Chain plates look fine with the exception of one to port. These and other hull fittings such as seacocks are grounded.

Running rigging is manilla, condition doubtful for active sailing. Sails were new in 1956, but were not available for inspection. There are two anchors aboard--one 100 pound and one 125 pound kedge with two shots of perfectly good 1/2" galvanized chain.

As you know this vessel is (or has been until very recently) in sailing condition. In our estimation she is currently in better condition than almost anything the Seaport now owns. She is a good looking boat and one that would be a great asset to the Seaport especially in view of the fact that she was Noank-built. Like the MODESTY, she will need attention as soon as she arrives, for the rot in her bulwarks and covering boards will spread as fast as it did in the BOWDOIN. Her bottom will need no attention for some time, for it has been carefully gone over by an expert caulker and repainted.

Very truly yours

PALMER SERVICE INC.

Henry R. Palmer, Jr.

Appendix V

1969 Log of the return of the *Emma C. Berry* to Mystic, by Arthur Krause.

Saturday, June 14, 1969:
Maynard Bray, Shipyard Supervisor at the Seaport, his wife Anne and daughter Kathy headed for Bay Head, New Jersey in the Seaport's utility boat *TWO BROTHERS* to prepare the *BERRY* for her voyage to Mystic. Neglected for three years, she needed paint, new rigging, and a good cleaning.

Friday, June 20:
After three days of furious painting by the Brays, the *BERRY* had begun to look like her old self as she was towed up the Inland Waterway to Manasquam Inlet, with Slade Dale as pilot. The rest of the *BERRY's* crew arrived Friday evening; Paul Bates and Victor Burdick of Noank, Charles Haines of Mystic, Arthur Krause of Chester, Connecticut and Michael Sturges and Frank Young of the Seaport staff. Near midnight Chester Patterson of Stonington arrived with his power boat *NIGHT HAWK*. With David Finley of Canton, Ohio as crew, *NIGHT HAWK* was to tow the *BERRY* to Mystic.

Saturday, June 21:
A raw day with a strong northeast breeze and heavy sea running outside, making it too risky to get underway. "Blight" Bray turned his crew to reeving off new running rigging, bending sails and rattling down. During the afternoon, *NIGHT HAWK* assisted the Coast Guard in making a hair-breadth rescue of four persons whose boat had capsized to windward of the inlet jetty. Even Charlie and Paul, who turned out to be resourceful ship's cooks, were too tired to go ashore.

Sunday, June 22:
A magnificent day with a fresh dry northeaster, but the sea still running too high to tow. The crew set to work scraping the masts and painting the deckhouses, and knocked off in the afternoon to explore a few miles of the Inland Waterway. Towards evening the wind veered to the southeast and moderated, hence the decision to get underway at daybreak.

Monday, June 23:
With a moderate breeze 4:00 a.m. the *BERRY* made ready for sea. The anchor was aweigh at 6:15 and towed by *NIGHT HAWK*, the *BERRY* eased through the inlet surges into the open sea. Once clear of the inlet all sail was set and a course shaped for Sandy Hook. With an increasing breeze New Jersey's beach pavilions sped by like picket fence posts, and just past ten the mainsail

was taken in for the dead run up Ambrose Channel to the Verrazano Bridge. All sail was taken in for the tow up the East River, as the wind was dead on and coming on to blow. With *NIGHT HAWK* dodging oil and railroad barges and a strong favoring current, the *BERRY* set a sailing record from the Battery to Hells Gate that no New York taxi driver would ever dare to equal.

Once past Throgs Neck and with a favoring slant, the crew made sail again. While the *NIGHT HAWK* refueled, the *BERRY* sailed on her own out past Execution Rocks. The tow was soon resumed and at three *AMERICA* passed to windward almost hidden in the drizzle.

As the wind backed suddenly into the northeast and began to kick up a nasty chop, the *BERRY's* 103 years began to tell, and she started to leak at an alarming rate. Engineer Burdick has to start his gasoline pumps every fifteen minutes, and when the backup pump refused to start, *NIGHT HAWK* headed her charge for Stamford.

A slightly dispirited and soggy crew faced a long night of pumping to keep the old girl afloat. But the Yacht Haven Marina took the schooner alongside for the night and provided two electric bilge pumps. No sooner had the ship been secured than the two ship's cooks disappeared over the rail lured by prospects of roast beef and dry socks provided by Charlie's sister. After one of Chester Patterson's superb chowders the crew almost didn't mind the prospect of sleeping in soaked sleeping bags in soggy clothes.

Tuesday, June 24:
A layover was in order until a reliable backup pump could be delivered from Mystic Seaport. Around eleven the wayward ship's cooks appeared and were sent ashore again to commandeer Charlie's sister's sewing machine to manufacture a magnificent twenty-foot homeward bound pennant out of old signal flags. Anne Bray and Betsy Sturges arrived with a replacement pump around one, and in a flat calm to tow to the eastward was resumed. A few miles out of Stamford, the *TWO BROTHERS* had engine failure. While Sturges and Krause tried every trick but the right one and had thoughts of spending the night drifting on Long Island Sound, the *BERRY* and *NIGHT HAWK* disappeared into the fog. Before long *NIGHT HAWK* came charging back to rescue, and for a while she had both the *BERRY* and her errant co-escort in tow.

With thickening visibility the procession put into Black Rock for the night. The Fayerweather Yacht Club really turned to and allowed the *BERRY* to lay alongside their float for the night and provided electric pumps as well as full courtesies for the crew. A local boatyard owner presented the *BERRY* with several bags of sawdust for her seams, and a mascot, a little black kitten-- Little Emma--for her crew.

Wednesday, June 25:

Being dead down wind from the Bridgeport dump gave all hands real impetus to be off for Mystic at 7 a.m. *NIGHT HAWK* heads the *BERRY* into the moderate easterly under threatening skies. Encouraging Little Emma to find her sea legs occupied the crew, plus Mystic Seaport researcher, John Kochiss, for most of the uneventful tow up the Sound. Arriving off the Mystic River at 4:30 p.m. the crew made sail for the last time to sail the *BERRY* up the river with the faithful pump spouting water almost steadily. Many turned out along the riverside to welcome the old girl to her final home. At 6:15 the last lines were passed to the dock on Seaport Street and the *BERRY* was home to rest after 103 years of faithful service.

Appendix VI

Staff who worked on the Museum restorations and the 1992 sea trials

1969-71
Ship Carpenters: Arnold Crossman, shipwright in charge of the restoration, Irving Holdredge, Howard Davis, Mark Thackston, Willits Ansel
Rigger: Robert Boulware
Painter: Malcolm Stewart
Caulker: Bert LeBlanc

1987-88
Ship Carpenters: Kevin Dwyer, shipwright in charge of the restoration, Roger Hambidge, Jeff Pearson, Arnold Crossman, Howard Davis, Tom Jannke, Pat Nelson, Bill Cochrane, Chris Rawlings, David Snediker
Painters: Esta Greenfield, Lauren Hart, Mary Allen Marcott, Annie Oosterwyk, Allison Pyott
Sawyer: Maurice Baron
Caulker: Basil Tuplin
Iron Work: Ron Anderson, Clint Wright
Riggers: Gary Adair, Karl Robinson, Dean Seder
Sailmaker: Donald Lucas
Draftsmen: Robert Allyn, Larry Jacobsen, Steen Kokborg, Dan Marcus
Research and Documentation: Nancy d'Estang

1992 Sea Trial
Captain: Quentin Snediker

Project Volunteers
Bill Dinan, Bob Watt, Damion Reardon, Larry Jacobsen, Donald Lucas, Rebecca Waters, John Goetsch, John Lease, Holly David, and the Gung Ho Squad

ACKNOWLEDGMENTS

I am indebted to those who preserved, researched, recorded, and photographed the *Emma C. Berry*, allowing me to create a compendium of her incredible life story and of the people who were intimate with her throughout her years. Countless Noank and area residents have also contributed to my understanding and appreciation of this important piece of maritime history.

Willits Ansel's *Restoration of the Smack Emma C. Berry* traces the first phase of renovations begun in 1969 and offers important insights into her construction details. I'm grateful to him for allowing me to use his sketches for this book.

Sam Merrick's biography of Slade Dale, who owned the *Berry* the longest and gifted her to the Seaport, is full of first-hand accounts and articles by Mr. Dale regarding his long-held interest in the *Berry* and his use of her as a charter and coasting schooner.

The *Work Progress Handbook*, compiled by Nancy d'Estang, records all known repairs to the *Berry* since her construction in 1866. I'm grateful that while this manuscript was being edited I could refer to it to make sure my facts were correct. It was due to Nancy's comprehensive nomination document that the *Emma C. Berry* was awarded National Historic Landmark status in 1994.

Arnold Crossman was lead shipwright during the *Berry's* first reconstruction, and his intimate knowledge of the *Berry's* construction details, and willingness to share that knowledge, was invaluable.

Kevin Dwyer's unpublished manuscript, *Noank Well Smacks and the Fishing Industry*, provides a wealth of information on the Noank fishing fleet of the mid-to-late 1800s places the *Berry* in a historical and economic context that is extremely useful in both understanding her role in an enormous enterprise, and grasping the truly fortuitous circumstances that led her to be the last surviving vessel of her kind. Kevin was the Principal on the *Berry's* second reconstruction, and thanks to his research regarding what type of work the shipwrights had done during the first reconstruction, I was able to develop a correct sail plan.

Numerous colleagues from Mystic Seaport assisted me tremendously with Collections and Research access, among them Paul O'Pecko, Maribeth Bielinski, Carol Mowrey, Mindy Matheson, Pat Wilbur, and Kane Borden from the Shipyard's Documentation Shop.

Slade Dale's hundreds of photographs of the *Berry* were willed to John Van Horn, Jr., who opened his archive to me. He was of immeasurable assistance in sending me rarely-seen photos of the *Berry* and other boats owned by Dale, sharing stories of those days, and connecting us with others who remembered *Emma* in days gone by.

I would also like to acknowledge the help and support of the Noank Historical Society for the use of their extensive document archive and reference material. Board, staff members, and volunteers including Mary Anderson, Elizabeth Boucher, Nancy d'Estang, Elizabeth duRocher, Jennifer Emerson, Shirley McFadden, Arnold Crossman, Paul Bates, Norman Brouwer, Jim Giblin, Bryan, Kathleen, and Victor Burdick, and George Hohenstein provided cheerful and continuous support as I worked on this manuscript.

Thank you to Dr. John E. Kelly III for his generous support for the book's publication, and to Mike Kelly for his enthusiastic interest in the *Patience* history.

Maynard Bray, maritime historian, formerly head of watercraft preservation at Mystic Seaport and longtime technical editor at *WoodenBoat* magazine, was kind enough to offer his expertise and editorial insight as I developed the first draft.

Louisa Alger Watrous, Intellectual Property Manager at Mystic Seaport and volunteer archivist and Member, Publications Committee at Noank Historical Society, provided invaluable help with research over the years, as the liaison between the NHS and MSM collections, and working with John Van Horn, Jr. on the photographs from his F. Slade Dale Collection.

Markham Starr, my book designer and former Mystic Seaport colleague, transformed my manuscript and photos into a beautiful layout.

Penny Newbury, my editor, deserves very special thanks as our "book angel" for her dedicated efforts in working with the team on all the small details, with a commitment that has brought this book into being.

And truly, I could not have completed this project without the loving support and encouragement of my wife Betty, who has been my faithful partner for 73 years.

BIBLIOGRAPHY

Ansel, Willits D. *The Restoration of the Smack* Emma C. Berry *at Mystic Seaport*, 1969-1971. The Marine Historical Association, Inc., Mystic, CT. 1973.

Caulkins, Frances Manwaring. *History of New London, Connecticut*. New London: H.D. Utley, 1895.

Chapelle, Howard I. *The National Watercraft Collection*. Washington, DC: U.S. Government Printing Office, 1960.

Dale, Slade. "Old *Emma* Comes to Barnegat, Part I." *Yachting*, 1932. Rpt. in *Slade Dale: the Life of His Choice*. Sam Merrick. Toms River, NJ: Ocean County Historical Society, 1998. Print. 116-120.

Dale, Slade. "Old *Emma* Comes to Barnegat, Part II." *Yachting,* 1933. Rpt. in *Slade Dale: the Life of His Choice*. Sam Merrick. Toms River, NJ: Ocean County Historical Society, 1998. Print. 121-126.

d'Estang, Nancy. *Emma C. Berry Work Progress Handbook: Record of Known Work 1866 to 1995*. Mystic Seaport Museum, Inc., 1995.

Dwyer, Kevin, and d'Estang, Nancy. *The Restoration of the Emma C. Berry and the History of the Noank Smacks. 1993-1994.* Unpublished manuscript. Mystic Seaport Museum, Inc., Mystic, CT.

Dwyer, Kevin, and d'Estang, Nancy. *The Connecticut Smack Emma C. Berry: her research and restoration 1969-1971* and 1987-1988. 1993-1994. TS. Mystic Seaport Museum, Inc., Mystic, CT.

Dwyer, Kevin. *Noank Well Smacks and the Fishing Industry.* Unpublished manuscript. Mystic Seaport Museum, Inc., Mystic, CT, 1989.

Edey, Maitland. "Sea Dog Eat Sea Dog." *LIFE* magazine, July 3, 1962.

Knapp, Edward Everett. *The Smacks of Noank.* Unpublished manuscript. Mystic Seaport Museum, Inc., Mystic, CT, G.W. Blunt White Library, Coll. 171, 1931.

Krause, Arthur. "The *Emma C. Berry*, June 5, 1866—" in *The Log of Mystic Seaport,* Vol. 21, Number 1. Mystic: Mystic Seaport Museum, Inc., September 1969, 86-90.

Merrick, Sam. *F. Slade Dale: the Life of His Choice.* Ocean County Historical Society, Toms River, NJ, 1998.

Palmer, Robert. Interviewed by Nancy d'Estang, Kevin Dwyer, and Dean Seder. *Regarding Noank smacks, their construction and rigging.* Mystic Seaport Museum Shipyard, Mystic, CT, 1986-1992.

Peterson, William. *Mystic Built: Ships and Shipyards of the Mystic River, Connecticut 1784-1919.* Mystic, CT: Mystic Seaport Museum, Inc., 1989.

Rathbun, Benjamin. *Captains B.F. Rathbun of Noank.* Noank, CT: Noank Historical Society, 1997.

Rathbun, Ben, Mary Anderson, Arnold Crossman and Jim Giblin. Noank: *Celebrating a Maritime Heritage: Meeting of the Square Riggers at Cape Horn, Henry Davis and Cleopatra's Needle, Noank Boatshops, Noank Maritime History, The Revised Papers of Claude Chester.* Noank Historical Society, Inc., 2002.

Shields, Cornelius. *Cornelius Shields on Sailing.* Prentice-Hall, 1964.

Stark, Charles R. *Groton: 1705-1905.* Stonington, CT: Palmer Press, 1922.

Tilton, George Fred. *Cap'n George Fred" Himself.* 1st copyright 1927. 1st printing Edgartown, MA: Dukes County Historical Society, 1969.

Thornton, W. George. *Emma's Epic*. 1966. TS. Rochester, New York.

United States National Museum Bulletin #219. Washington, D.C.: The Smithsonian Institution, *National Watercraft Collection, 1960*. *https://repository.si.edu/bitstream/handle/10088/10043/USNMB_2191960_ unit.pdf.txt*.

Unknown. *Merchant Vessels of the United States*. Washington, D.C.: Bureau of Navigation, 1920. *http://archive.org/stream/merchantvessels04guar-goog/merchantvessels04guargoog_djvu.txt*.

For Further Reading and Reference

I know of no better first-hand account of Noank than Edward Everett Knapp's unpublished 1931 manuscript, *The Smacks of Noank*, written in the colorful vernacular characteristic of many of the area's elder maritime statesmen and containing troves of researched information on the history of the borough from its settlements to its fishing fleets to its "present day" activities. It also contains an equal measure of overheard yarns, first and second-hand anecdotes, and shrewd observations. It is well worth anyone's time to seek it out in the G.W. Blunt White Library at Mystic Seaport and spend a day with Everett and his delightful style.

For anyone wishing to review and understand the inordinate amount of research, information and organization of materials that went into the restoration of the *Berry,* I recommend the exhaustive 1995 *Works Progress Log* compiled and written by Nancy d'Estang. This manual includes a comprehensive bibliography of historical manuscripts, newspaper clippings, first-hand accounts, maritime history, and books focusing on well smacks, their construction and use throughout history.

Helpful Websites

Mystic Seaport: *http://www.mysticseaport.org*

Noank Historical Society: *http://www.noankhistoricalsociety.org*

Ships Nostalgia: *http://www.shipsnostalgia.com* (discussions of various meanings of sloop vs. smack)

Bay Head Historical Society: *http://www.bayheadhistoricalsociety.com/about.php*

John Van Horn, Jr.'s, F. Slade Dale Photo Collection and photography: *http://www.johnvanhornphotos.com*

Ocean County Historical Society, Toms River, New Jersey: *http://www.oceancountyhistory.org/publications/*

Noank Historical Society plans to issue a Second Edition of the book in 2016. We welcome any additional photos, facts, anecdotes, or clarifications from readers regarding the *Emma C. Berry* and her colorful history. Please send all material and contact information to Noank Historical Society, PO Box 9454, Noank, CT 06340 or by email to: noankhist@global.net.

INDEX

Palmer, Robert, Deacon   19,21
Palmer, Robert (Jr.)   34
Palmer, Ear   18
Palmer, Emma C. Berry   8,11,21,83
Palmer, Henry   75
Palmer, John   19
Palmer, Roswell   8
Palmer, Roswell (Jr.)   8
Palmer Yard (R&J)   19,24,34
Peerless engine   15,49,54
Patience   57,58,59,60,85,101
Phebe   21
Philadelphia, Pennsylvania   60
Pilot boat   21
Plum Island, New York   31,32
Point Pleasant, New Jersey   75
Postscript 46,54,58,64
Potter, Walton 37
Pronto 24
Purchase price 41
R&J Palmer yards 19,24,34
R. Palmer &Sons 25
Railroad ties transport 60
Rathbun, Calvin 15
Reconstruction 51,52,85,88,101
Registration 24
Restoration 11,22,23,28,29,41,51,61,69,71,76,78,79,80,82
85,87,99,100,106
Rigging 12,16,28,36,41,77,80,86,96,104
Robbie F. Sylvester 25,84
Robert Palmer & Sons 25,34
Rockland, Maine 15,41
Rogers, Henry 24,34
Rogers, Thomas 24,34
Sail cringle 85
Sail plan 12,50,101
Sails 12,15,16,20,22,35,41,50,67
Savannah, Georgia 27

About the Author

Lawrence "Larry" R. Jacobsen is a near-lifelong resident of Groton and Mystic, Connecticut and had a long and varied career in the shipbuilding and design business. He served in the U.S. Navy from 1943 to 1946, in the Pacific. Larry is a retired naval architect and Connecticut Licensed Professional Engineer. He was a Chief Hull and Structures Designer in the Electric Boat Division of General Dynamics in Groton, Connecticut. He finished his career there as a Submarine Tanker Development Program Manager. Upon his retirement he worked as a marine draftsman and engineer at the Mystic Seaport Henry B. duPont Preservation Shipyard Documentation Shop from 1985 to 2012, and was the Mystic Seaport Noyes Volunteer of the Year in 2010. His drawings of the *Emma C. Berry* and other major vessel drawings in the Watercraft Collection are part of the Daniel S. Gregory Ships Plans Library at Mystic Seaport.

For years, Larry was a boat owner and avid sailor, participating in many sailing races on Long Island Sound, and in the annual Bermuda Races. Larry has been involved with the Sound Inter Club sailboat restoration project since 2010 (www.soundinterclub.org), advising on the boat design and saving stories of the day. He is currently researching a book of historic homes and buildings in Noank for the 50th anniversary of the Noank Historical Society in 2016, and on Connecticut railroad and banking magnate Morton Plant and the over forty yachts owned by Plant and his son, Henry. Larry lives in Mystic, Connecticut with his wife Betty.

Made in the USA
Middletown, DE
05 July 2018